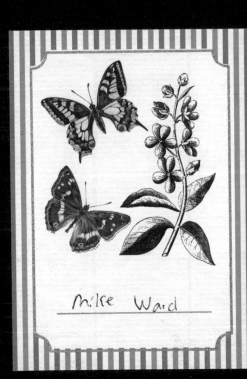

Mike Ward

I Am the Wolf

I Am the Wolf

Lyrics and Writings

MARK LANEGAN

DA CAPO PRESS

Da Capo Press
Hachette Book Group
1290 Avenue of the Americas, New York, NY 10104
www.dacapopress.com
Printed in the United States of America

First Edition: August 2017
Published by Da Capo Press, an imprint of Perseus Books, LLC, a subsidiary of
Hachette Book Group, Inc.
The Hachette Speakers Bureau provides a wide range of authors for speaking events.
To find out more, go to www.hachettespeakersbureau.com or call (866) 376-6591.

The publisher is not responsible for websites (or their content) that are not owned by
the publisher.

Print book interior design by Jeff Williams

Library of Congress Cataloging-in-Publication Data
Names: Lanegan, Mark.
Title: I am the wolf : lyrics and writings / Mark Lanegan.
Other titles: Lyrics.
Description: Boston, MA : Da Capo Press, [2017]
Identifiers: LCCN 2017003201| ISBN 9780306825279 (hardcover) | ISBN
9780306825286 (ebook)
Classification: LCC ML54.6.L19 L9 2017 | DDC 782.42166092—dc23
LC record available at https://lccn.loc.gov/2017003201

ISBNs: 978-0-306-82527-9 (hardcover), 978-0-306-82528-6 (ebook)

LSC-C

10   9   8   7   6   5   4   3   2

Contents

Preface by John Cale

A VOICE is your first passport. You reach people with whatever noise you find effective. Then come the words that glom you to your listener like an invisible umbilical cord, each word a scramble with its own history that you throw like dice into the lake—but this is Mark Lanegan's lake and each time the songs writhe in the water you hear the light and the darkness that illuminate him.

When reading Mark's lyrical thoughts, it's impossible for a person to tune out the voice that burrows deep inside. Of course, separation is possible, but an unnecessary step to understand the infinite stages of soul-searching crafted within the penned thoughts of raging gentility that is Mark Lanegan.

There is darkness here for sure, but it is a mark of toleration. As someone who has tolerated an affection for darkness there is his own unique need to be educated by it—show me how many levels of dark you have and we can codify them for our conversation and admire them for their variety. This education is not a way of explaining your devils away. It is the reflection of how we care for pain. It is not there to punish us for our history of carelessness, but to illuminate the debris of our affections.

Singing has this way of illuminating the debris—we breathe out the melodies that we are allowed to inhale—as if a calculus of our breathing is a prerequisite for listening. We breathe as we listen. We breathe *better* as we listen. That is the value of songs. They help us breathe.

I don't mean to imply that subconsciously we are drowning in a silent world. We have survived that and now clamber ahead into our conversations in whatever form they occur—the blind leading the blind—deaf to ourselves, but singing so we can be heard.

Mark has this quality in his voice—you can find spring, summer, fall, and winter around the corners of the words. Those who listen and those who sing are grateful for these corners to look around.

—JOHN CALE
Los Angeles, February 2017

Foreword by Moby

WHEN LOOKING at Mark Lanegan's lyric poems you see just how quick and willing he is to throw himself under the bus. Quick and willing but with an almost delicate resignation, as if under the bus is his natural resting place. Under the bus is home.

Reading these lyric poems—a life's work—you start to feel as if you're watching a time lapse of darkening weather. The storms come in and the storms go out and sometimes they rage, but in the end we're becalmed. And there's Mark, sitting in his formerly drunken boat, a wry smile on his face.

Good, have I done good?

You want to say, "Yes, you've done good." Even Jesus with his little starry crown probably thinks so.

Through the waves of darkness and the literal and metaphoric bottoming out there exists a sweetness, a kindness for the reader and the listener—and sometimes even for the writer/singer. But usually the self-directed mercy is strained, as if the writer's shortcomings are beyond forgiveness.

No redemption in the cards.

But there is, probably.

> *He came in this world alone*
> *Spent all his time alone*
> *He left this life alone*

Again, Jesus. But the writer/singer, too. Mark's Jesus, and the Jesus and writer/singer of Leonard Cohen's "Suzanne." A baffled, existential Jesus, showing up as us, staring into the void, and going quietly and sadly into the good night.

This lifetime of work ages, just as the writer/singer ages. By the end of this collection some of the rage has abated, some of the violence softened. But there's a thread, a through line, walking quietly from the first line to the last: that the world is sad, that the world is unknowable, and that the world has hurt and will hurt you, but there's also an unspeakable luminous beauty in the world and in how we live through it.

> *The stars and the moon*
> *Aren't where they're supposed to be*

And there's that other through line: liquor and drugs. This is how Mark and I met, at an event for people who'd ended up loving liquor and drugs a bit too much.

When you've been at the bottom you end up humbled. And humiliated, broken by the choice between delusion and sickness and death or honesty and humility and some type of life. Mark has chosen honesty and humility and some type of life, and the honesty and the humility inform all of these words and songs.

> *You don't love me*
> *What's to love, anyway?*

The cry of the broken, as if to say, "Why would I bother to live? Life is wasted on me." But somehow, strangely, we end up alive when our betters are long dead.

Every addict has woken up at some point and thought, nonplussed and disappointed, "Why am I still alive?" But we're alive. Oddly. Somehow. And as we come back to some semblance of sanity and life we always remember our debasements and horrors and viciousness and fear. And it informs everything we are and end up being. Hopefully. But underneath there's still the self-doubt, the plague of the knowledge that we're lesser than.

My favorite lines in Mark's lyric poem book are these:

> *I'm sorry*
> *I'm sorry*
> *I'm sorry*

It's what we say to everyone. To ourselves. To the people who raised us. To the people who've loved us. To God.

> *I'm sorry*

And through these beautiful words there's honesty and grace and humility and even some libido. But underneath is that sweet refrain.

> *I'm sorry*

We could've done better. We could've been better. We're sorry.

> *My sin is done, and it won't be forgiven*

But it will, it has, and somehow, somewhere we know the truth of that.

—MOBY
Los Angeles, March 2017

Acknowledgments

I'D LIKE to thank Ben Schafer, Shelley Brien, Kevin Gasser, Laurie Davis, John Dee, Steve Strange, Robby Fraser, Sean Wheeler, Roberto Bentivegna, Cleon Peterson, Alain Johannes, Jeff Barrett, Roger Trust, Jonathan Poneman, Bob Pfeifer, Martin Feveyear, Mike Johnson, Greg Dulli, John Agnello, Christopher Paulson, Duke Eriksen, Teo Bicchieri, Trina Lanegan, Paolo Bicchieri, David Coppin Lanegan, Steve Gullick, Gary Lee Conner, Anna Hrnjak, Joy Lessard, Rob Marshall, Remco Frijns, Frederic Lyenn Jacques, Jean-Philippe De Gheest, Clay Decker, Jeff Fielder, Dave Rosser, Ava Stroud, Emily Mackey, Sonny Garwood, Aldo Struyf, and all the musicians who have played with me, inspired me, and showed me how to make music.

Introduction

THIS BOOK is a collection of song lyrics. When I was a kid, music, books, and films were my saviors, but I never thought I would actually play or write anything myself . . . like most things in life I fell into it by accident and at first the only motivation for being creative was an intense, restless dissatisfaction in the way I felt and an attempt to change it. The reason I pumped gas at Texaco, cleaned restrooms, washed dishes and cooked breakfast at truck stops, repossessed TVs and appliances, moved furniture, painted houses, sold drugs, used drugs, tried to join the circus, tried to join the army, drank alcohol until blackout time after time, got into confrontations with strangers over real or imagined slights, entered into countless doomed and dysfunctional relationships, stole things, sold things I stole, had sex wherever possible, and walked a seemingly endless nonsensical parade acting out in either secretive or public ways was the same reason I joined a band. The opportunity presented itself, I said yes, and then sometimes quickly, sometimes slowly, and on many occasions painfully, I learned how to do it. I've never been very smart, just lucky.

—MARK LANEGAN
Los Angeles

The Winding Sheet

(1989)

My HOUSEMATES and I referred to it as the waiting area at a morgue. It was cold and damp in the sparsely furnished, too brightly lit front room. Loveseat, chair, turntable, heavily stained white carpet, shitty space heater, and light bulb. I happened to glance through the doorway and saw a huge rat standing in the kitchen staring nonchalantly back at me and suddenly realized where the infestation of fleas in the place was coming from. It was 1989 and although I had been playing rock music for a few years, I was still working stultifying, dead-end jobs and was totally unmotivated and directionless about the future. At the pinnacle of my underachievement as an indie singer with Screaming Trees, Sub Pop Records offered me a solo deal, and that became the catalyst for my interest in songwriting. Prior to this I had sometimes written words with the other members of my first band or, more often, had tried to change their lyrics to fit me in a more personal way. This was a tedious, frustrating routine that was never enjoyable, and so *The Winding Sheet* became my first attempt at going it alone.

Since writing songs also meant playing guitar for the first time, my roommate Dylan Carlson showed me a chord progression that I used in about half the tunes, and Mike Johnson of the Eugene, Oregon, band Snakepit put intros, outros, and middle sections to them, becoming my primary accomplice and advisor in the process. The recording was made by legendary Northwest producer Jack Endino at Reciprocal Studio in three or four days, with him constantly assuring me that what we were doing was not terrible. The title for the record came from something I heard Maya Angelou say on a PBS television program, and inspiration for the songs was born of sadness and uncertainty with my circumstances at the time: relationships, money problems, alcohol, depression, addiction, and so on. Sometimes serious, sometimes comical. Other motivations included the endless gray, rain-saturated days of Seattle and a preoccupation with death as well as an ever-pervasive sense of impending doom . . . feel-good stuff. Musical influence came from a love of the blues and of the introspective and poetic bent of Leonard Cohen, John Cale, Jeffrey Lee Pierce, Falling James Moreland, Ian Curtis, Nick Cave, and local Portland, Oregon, heroes Chris Newman and Greg Sage.

Mockingbirds

Your voice is a mockingbird
Calling me when the day is done
You please yourself with every word
Telling me where I'm going wrong
Telling me where I've gone wrong

Get me out, it's starting to burn
I can't let go for the life of me
Some hold tighter and some turn
Another fire out in front of me
My whole life out in front of me

You can't kill what's already dead
But I don't blame you for trying it
The sun comes up and falls away
Two little birds making sense of it
Two mockingbirds making sense of it

Museum

You hear them call your name
From your room far removed
Don't let them use you in every way, stay unchained
Around and 'round you go
They'll never know what you've seen

Why have you turned away?
You can't believe, believe in me
Couldn't you try one time
To see through mine for a while?
It's a solitary star
Shining precious light, light on me

When I see your eyes
They tell me what you find
But I ought to know by now

Did you hear them call your name
From your room, far removed?
I'd only use you in every way, stay unchained
It's a solitary star
Shining precious light, light on me

Undertow

Water will forgive me, I'm just trying to forget
Staring at the water as the waves turn ruby red
Remembering
Fear and paranoia run together in my dreams
Water will accept me and give me a peace I've never seen
Remembering

Wrap your arms around me
And I'm as light as anything
Push through the air I can't breathe
Your lips form a curious smile

Water will forgive me for everything I never should
Water will accept me for everything I never could

Wrap your arms around me
And I'm as light as anything
Push through the air I can't breathe

Ugly Sunday

I feel your blood run cold, and it's a rainy Sunday morning
I'll count the million miles I'm drifting from here to hell today
Behind their windows people stare, can't recognize the kindness there
Just prayers for drowning ships at sea
None for me and you

It'll take a hard rain to wash your taste away
Still I wish there was a reason left to stay

I'm drunk half-blind, and it's an ugly Sunday morning
The wind arrives with the clouds refusing to break apart
Like me
Why if all the world stopped turning
How can all this rain keep falling?
Washing me a million miles away from you
Why if I am so alone now
Is it getting hard to say goodbye now?
Goodbye
Goodbye

Down in the Dark

Baby, you're going down in the dark
Sure, my lonely night is falling
And I don't have very long
Think my blood might boil
Within my veins, might burn
And you're gonna make it better for a little while

Baby, you're gonna die someday
See you when you're crawling, wasted
Until you start to fade
Laugh when we start sinking faster
I wouldn't wait so long
It won't get any easier in the dawn

But you will
You will
You will
You will

Baby, you're going down in the dark
Believe my lonely night is falling
I don't have very long
Think my blood might boil
Within my veins, might burn
And you're gonna make it better for a little while

Wildflowers

I have to watch you come back to earth
Now it's all I can do
Will you still be convinced wildflowers
Are waiting for you?
In my mind I've done good things and never cared why
And my mind is an open door with nothing inside

Looks like the autumn is upon us
It's turning so cold
When everything said is either faded out
Or written in stone
If you could find an easier road, you'd take it today
You could have taken me anywhere
You just take it away

I have to watch you come back to earth
If it's all I can do
Will you still be convinced wildflowers
Are waiting for you?
Have we ever done good things and never cared why?
My mind is an open door with nothing inside

Eyes of a Child

See through the eyes of a child, and it won't be real
Eyes neither hateful or cruel
No lies concealed
Eyes that wander, eyes that stray
While the shame in your heart remains

Crying were the eyes of a child in pain tonight
Tears that have bled on you
From the heart of an angel of fear tonight
We can wander, we can stray
But the shame remains

See through the eyes of a child and it won't be real
I have loved your eyes, neither hateful or cruel
No lies concealed
We could wander, we could stray
But the shame has remained
It has remained

The Winding Sheet

Saw god staring from the wall
I was alone and lost
Here to take me from this world
Still alone and lost

At night when the dogs from hell come out
And roam my house in chains of gold
The darkness dares my eyes to close

Saw a ghost in the shadows smile
I was sick in my soul
All tied up in a winding sheet
Still sick in my soul

At night when the dogs from hell come out
And roam my house in chains of gold
The darkness dares my eyes to close
With the setting sun

They tried to lay me back on thorns
Full of fear in my head
Lay me back so I could not rise
Full of fear in my head

At night when the dogs from hell come out
And roam my house in chains of gold
The darkness dares my eyes to close
Close with the setting sun

Woe

We got some poison in us
Cyanide and nicotine
More than you've ever seen
More than I can believe
Woe

Guns, guns, they all got guns
Now they wanna shoot someone
I'd rather be drunk than dead
Or go where jesus fled
So I'll get drunk again
Or maybe not
Woe

I saw on a tombstone
He came in this world alone
Spent all his time alone
He left this life alone
Woe

Ten Feet Tall

I can see they're coming
Just tell me it ain't true
All alone in sorrow and I
Fall back to you
One time or another like I thought
She is alone
And I don't walk that tall

Memories amounting to nothing I can keep
Just as soon forgotten
Hate is all that her tears ever show
Saying sing, come on black cat, sing
Hate is gold dripping lies from a tongue
Demanding all
I don't walk that tall

I see they're coming
Tell me it ain't true
Head down in sorrow
And I stumble back to you
One time or another you might find
Hate is all that her tears ever show
Saying sing, come on black cat, sing
I don't walk that tall

Juarez

Night train is groovy
And orange jubilee
Feels good coming and going
I'm warm all over me
Well, fire up the crack, boys
And tie off my arm
Cinch up my diaper
Turn the TV on
Give me another blowjob before I'm on the nod
Say you'll always love me
And never do me harm
Never do me harm

I Love You, Little Girl

I love you, little girl
Better than I love my
Better than I love myself

I want you here with me
Forever
Ever and ever

Just so far from home
Just so far from home

Love you, little girl
Love you, little girl

Whiskey for the Holy Ghost
(1990–1994)

I WAS drifting in and out of sleep with Van Morrison's *Astral Weeks* playing in the bedroom, and when I awoke had an epiphany: I needed to make a record that was much more expansive than *The Winding Sheet* and wanted to create something singular, with its own world inside it. Around this same time a girlfriend of mine gave me a copy of *Blood Meridian* by Cormac McCarthy, which sparked my imagination with its intense imagery. Morrison and McCarthy, those two disparate influences, became the signposts for *Whiskey*. From the time I began writing the songs until the record was done, Screaming Trees also wrote and recorded an album and did much touring, so I was compelled to work on my own record in the off-time. A week here, a month there—and what I had originally intended to be a quick recording experience stretched out over four years. Many different musicians, engineers, producers, and studios were burned through, and my behavior became erratic, not easy to deal with as I continually rewrote, re-recorded, and remixed tunes according to an internal, chemically cracked sensibility that sometimes verged on paranoia. Despite these self-inflicted setbacks, the resulting record came somewhat close to the vision I had in my Seattle bedroom, and some of the tunes became staples of my live set for years. "Carnival," one of the first songs recorded, is the most obviously influenced by

Van Morrison, and "Pendulum" started as a joke designed to make my musical partner Mike Johnson laugh. While recording "The River Rise" at a New York City studio just off Times Square, my friend J. Mascis was delighted to find a cookie jar whose lid was the head of a hobo that whistled when removed and said he'd give me $50 to put the sound on the recording. It's the first thing you hear on the album.

The River Rise

Oh, the river rise
And it's a mile high
Is this worth drawing?
Is this worth trying?
'Cause I could fall like a tear
There's nothing else I can do

When I'm not alone
Nothing's beside me
What one eye sees
The other's blinding
But I could fall just as if I were young
With a lifetime to think of you

Fire one for losing
And two for hiding
Keep river moving
Moving right by me
I could fall
If there's nothing else I can do

Oh, the river rise
And it's a mile high
Has this world drowned?
Has this world tried?
'Cause I could fall like a tear
There's nothing else I can do

Borracho

Trouble comes in slowly
An everlasting light come to shine all over me
Bright in the morning
Like all of heaven's love come to shine on me
And to you who never need
Fuck yourself
I need some more room to breathe

Here come the devil prowling around
One whiskey for every ghost
And I'm sorry for what I've done
'Cause it's me who knows what it cost
It breaks and it breeds and it tears you apart
It bites and it bleeds
And this desert turns to ocean over me
Here come the devil prowling around
One whiskey for every ghost
And I'm sorry for what I said
I said I just don't care anymore
A fool can feed on a notion
Sees and believes
And this desert turns to ocean over me

Trouble comes in slowly
An everlasting light come to shine all over me
At the dead end of morning
With all of heaven's love come to shine on me
The fool that feeds on a notion
Sees and believes
And this desert turns to ocean over me

Here come the devil buying a round
One whiskey for every ghost
And I'm sorry for what I done
Lord, it's me who knows what it cost
The fool that feeds on a notion
Sees and believes
And this desert turns to ocean over me
Here come the devil prowling around
One whiskey for every ghost
And I'm sorry for what I said
I said I just don't care anymore
It breaks and it breeds and it tears you apart
It bites and it bleeds
And this desert turns to ocean over me

House a Home

Here you are at the top of a tower
How could a body take that much?
Alone through every waking hour
Asleep without nobody to touch
Oh oh oh
There's only silence here
Oh oh oh
There's only silence here

And I'm not the one to make your house a home
Makes no sense to stay
Through another lonely last day
Oh no, baby, it's not right

Here you are crying in the night
How could a body take that much?
Find yourself standing outside
Where you ain't got nobody to touch
Oh oh oh
There's only silence here
Oh oh oh
There's only silence here

And I'm not the one to make your house a home
It makes no sense to stay
Through one more lonely last day
Oh no, baby, it's not right

Kingdoms of Rain

Are those halos in your hair or diamonds shining there?
Without a hope, without a prayer
This rain beats down like death
You turn your eyes to better men

Before I go, I'm hanging a cross on a nail
I hung one for you in there

Girl, lay your shame to rest
But hold the lies close to your breast
You stoop to feed the crows
Some scraps of truth already cold

Before I go, I'm hanging a cross on a nail
I hung one for you in there
In every kingdom a rain comes pouring down
'Cause I loved you so long
'Cause I loved you so long

Would you put halos in your hair?
Without a hope, without a prayer
With lies close to your breast
You finally lay your shame to rest

Before I go, I'm hanging a cross on a nail
I hung one for you in there
In every kingdom a rain comes pouring down
'Cause I loved you so long
'Cause I loved you so long

Carnival

Where in the world have you been?
It's as strange as I've ever lived
So you're coming along to the sideshow
I'll be falling all over like dominoes
For girls this sad in their eyes
They're all standing around being hypnotized
Then walking me back to the firing line
You smile to get in the door
They can't keep it closed anymore
Tell your ma that you're gone to the freakshow
I'm crawling all over the carnival
Just scratching a stitch in the skin
And I'm moaning for more of the medicine
In the morning you're wondering where you've been
Just turning your back to the ghost
And trying to look like you just might know
That all of the good that you've seen
Just went down and into the drain
A kiss in the street is all for now
In the morning I'm gonna find it on out
What in the world can it be?
It's a strange as I've ever seen
The girls are dead in their eyes
Just standing around like they're hypnotized
Who'll follow me back to the freakshow?
I'm crawling all over the carnival
And I am home

Riding the Nightingale

Dying mama
Barely breathing in a bed of nails
To wander through the ruins smoking and pale
I came upon an angel and a nightingale
Hanging where the darkness comes
Between the earth and skies above
Dead weight are my body's bones
I think I dug too deep a hole
Think I dug too deep a hole
Better run for cover, babe, you better hide
It don't do no good to wait 'til time decides
Time decides
Time
Time
I need a little more time

Riding on my nightingale
So many years too high
Riding my nightingale
Around my heart

Climbing down the stairs
The last step wouldn't touch me right
Well, you're too proud and I'm too spare
And I'm neither here nor there
It's only fear
Who'll open up the doors and let me breathe night air?
Better run for cover, babe, you better hide
It just don't do to wait 'til time decides
Time
Time
I need a little more time

Mama, I'm gonna cry now
Cry, I'm gonna cry now
You're making me cry now
Cry, I'm gonna cry now
Oh no no no no
I'm gonna cry
Cry
God knows I'm crying

Better run for cover, babe, you better hide
It just don't do to wait 'til time decides

Darling, I ride my nightingale
So many years too high
Flying my nightingale
Around my heart

Who's riding on my nightingale?
Who's riding on my nightingale?
I swear it's gonna bleed

El Sol

The sun is gone
And that's all I really know
No angels in the air
With hearts as good as gold
The closer you stand to the gates
The more the gates are closed

These darkened days
Make some bodies hunger and thirst
But blessed burns the sun
It's throwing shadows on the earth
The shadow you find at the gate
When all the gates are closed

Then in time you find your race is run
Felt much colder standing in the sun
Waiting for some warmth and coming down
Felt much older and then I really was
Waiting for some warmth and coming down

The sun is gone
Yeah, that's all I really know
No angels in the air
With hearts as good as gold
The closer you stand to the gates
The more the gates are closed

Then in time you find your race is run
Felt much colder standing in the sun
Waiting for some warmth and coming down
Felt much older and then I really was
Waiting for some warmth and coming down

Dead on You

You wear a ragged turquoise and twilight coat
I got my head hung down for you
Someday you're gonna need it
But it's worn where the cloth gets torn
And there's only one way to go
It's gone dead, dead
It's gone dead on you

Take off your ragged turquoise and twilight coat
I got my head hung down for you
Someday you're gonna need it
Well, it's worn where the cloth gets torn
And there's only one way to go
It's gone dead, dead
It's gone dead, dead
It's gone dead on you

Shooting Gallery

I'll tell you how I woke up on the line
Now, sister, I almost saw the light
Look, my hands are tied
I'll see you in another hallway
Some other time

And I don't understand this big parade
It's a five-star decoration day
Look, my hands are stained
I was washing them in the water
Where the water fell away

Tell you how I woke up on the line
Saw every soul in heaven passing by
Look, my hands are tied
I'll see you in another station
Some other time

Sunrise

Sunrise
Forgot to cover up my eyes
Sunrise
Should have covered up my eyes
Beauty wasted on me
Winds are shaking my tree
With a woman too good to believe
Take the first ride out that I see

Sunrise
Skies are serving my plan
Grounds are moving where I stand
Pull an airplane down with my hands
And take the first flight out that I can

Sunrise
Forgot to cover up my eyes
Beauty wasted on me
Winds are shaking my tree
With a woman too good to believe
Take the first ride out that I see
Sunrise

Pendulum

Jesus Christ been here and gone
What a painful price to pay
Left his life in a thunderstorm
With just cold dark eyes upon him
Swing pendulum, swing low
Got no place to call my own
Oh my lord, don't you bother me
I'm as tired as a man can be

Jesus Christ been here and gone
What a painful place to leave
There's frost on the limbs of a cherry tree
And this cold, cold wind is burying me
Swing pendulum, swing slow
Got no time to call my own
Oh my lord, don't you bother me
I'm as tired as a man can be
I'm as tired as a man can be

Judas Touch

Put out the lions and close the door
I need you more
Than I did before
Old Jack's been killed and buried away
Let's hang alone outside the gate
Flames scare the lions, as do their dreams
And that's the way it'll always be
Better close the door
That's the way it'll always be
Better close the door
Some fools forever don't ask for much
With frozen hand, calm Judas touch
Some towers of fire can be redeemed
Just let me burn
High worlds away

Beggar's Blues

Night train, silver moon
You ask me why I'm flying
To float on ashen wing
To choke on dust and feather
Oh moon, you are a liar
It's right we should pretend
And lie with one another
It's right we should be twins
For I have loved no other

Look for me, baby
I'm dragging loneliness and it's ten miles long
I thought I heard you scream, baby
In the wheels of a train that crawls where I don't wanna go
'Cause you forget me when I'm gone
Look for me, baby
Whenever ice is glistening upon the glass
Did you ever find your dream, baby?
Well, god knows I never held mine close enough
I watched them slip away like this

I've been from one end of this street to the other
Now I want the gift you promised me, lover
Look for me, baby
Crow flying by, we're sister and brother
Death is the kiss we give to one another
Look for me, baby
I'm dragging loneliness and it's ten miles long
I thought I heard you scream, baby
In the wheels of a train that crawls where I don't wanna go
'Cause you forget me when I'm gone

Night train, silver moon
You ask me why I'm flying
To float on ashen wing
To choke on dust and feather
My dreams will go no further
Won't calm my violent river
Guardian of peace
Let the beggar walk the winter

Look for me, baby
Look for me, baby

Scraps at Midnight

(1997–1998)

SHE ROLLED her eyes and said, "Always a lampshade, never a light," as I stumbled in loaded for the umpteenth time, and before long another love story lay dead in the ditch. Try as I might, it was becoming impossible to keep my head above the deluge, and by 1997, after a lengthy period of full-blown addiction and homelessness, I ended up in a halfway house in Pasadena, California, where I started writing the songs for *Scraps at Midnight* on a borrowed guitar. My trusted foil/cowriter/producer/ guitarist Mike Johnson came to town and stayed down the street at a run-down hotel, and we spent a couple of days in his room there trying to compose an album. Instead, most of our time was spent coming up with elaborate comedy scenarios that ultimately led nowhere. Eventually, we managed to put a tune together by taking a Bee Gees song apart and playing it backward ("Stay"), and he gave me the music for another ("Last One in the World"). A further three were written with my neighbor, an eccentric, big-hearted force of nature named Keni Richards. He had been the drummer in the 1980s band Autograph and was now a painter, but still owned a small Casio keyboard and created beautiful, seasick lullabies with it ("Bell Black Ocean," "Praying Ground"). One night while we were listening to Roxy Music, the CD began to skip and he duplicated the sound on his Casio, and that became the basis for another song ("Because of This"). Recording took place at the storied Rancho de la Luna in Joshua Tree, California, where a conversation with mystical owner Fred Drake gave me the lyrics for "Praying Ground," and my lifelong friendship with co-owner David Catching was to begin.

The minimal lyrics to "Hospital Roll Call" came from an unpleasant eight-day stay at a decrepit infirmary hallway in Montreal. Sixteen wasn't a room number, just what was written in black marker on the wall above my gurney. "Last One in the World" was not written about Kurt Cobain, as some have speculated, but for my friend Layne Staley, who was still living at the time. I loved them both as family: Kurt like a little brother, Layne like a twin.

Hospital Roll Call

Sixteen

Hotel

From the dime down to the well
Usually I fall and tell myself
It doesn't matter anyway
That this is just another day
I don't speak the truth too much
I hear the roar and the hush
And the cold chill of time
And I'm happy murdering my mind
I remember your voice
Turning around and around and around in my head
Now it's just like you said, everything inside is dead

From the pillar to the post
I kill what I can and miss the most
Of the blame when you get touched
Another town, another torch
Thought I saw you in a dream
Fill the hours in between when I call myself alone
And when I disappear below
I remember your face
But it's been a long, been a long, been a long, long day
And what I did along the way
Well, I wouldn't care to say

Stay

The heart will pound until the breath is gone
You know what I love, so put me on
When something has badly gone wrong with me
Living's not hard, it's just not easy always keeping the dogs off
Down like the rain
Down like the rain
Coming down like the rain
Coming down
I wanna be there by your side
'Cause this feels like dying, baby
Let me stay around
Let me stay around

You take my heart and my breath is gone
You know what I love, so put me on
Feel a little lightheaded, you know I'd have to be
Believing's not hard, it's just not easy staying blind to the obvious
Down like the rain
Down like the rain
Coming down like the rain
Coming down
I wanna be there by your side
'Cause this feels like dying, baby
Let me stay around
Let me stay around

Bell Black Ocean

We came to walk on this boulevard, love
Don't care where we're going
While it's true in time we might close our eyes
This won't die

Now we stop by the oceanside, love
You are all I see
And it isn't wrong that we don't belong
Anymore

We came to walk on this boulevard love
I don't care where we're going
While it's true in time we might close our eyes
This won't die

Last One in the World

Goodbye my friend, I hate to see you go
You brought me down a star
The last one in the world
I hear you cry, but let's not waste this night
The last one in the world

From within your lonely room
I hear you whisper, "See you soon"
I sense a dying spark
And watch you falling through the dark

Goodbye my friend, thank you for the dream
The last one in the world
I hear you cry, but let's not waste this night
The last one in the world

I listen to you call
And hardly hear you at all
Gonna walk the quiet night
And watch the river rolling by

The last one in the world
The last one in the world
The last one in the world

Wheels

Light ahead
Proves that the wheels broke down
Here I am still hanging on
Shadows only disappear
Just look around, there's no one here
A little spirit turned my light on out
And now can never be no doubt
You got to walk in the morning sun
And got to smile at everyone
Go, my love, on your way
To bigger and bright better days
And I'll go crazy for you, woman
And I won't stop loving you, baby
Oh yeah, here I am
Just feeling a little sad about it
Light ahead proves that the wheels broke down
Here I am still spinning round
Shadows only disappear
Just look around, there's no one here
A little spirit turned my light on out
And now can never be no doubt
I'm gonna wait 'til the stars come down
My little love's miles on her wing
For all the raindrop and tears not wasted
They been pouring down all day
I'm running 'round catching 'em, baby
I'm running 'round catching 'em, baby
Whichever way they fall
I won't stop loving you, baby
Whichever way you go
Oh yeah, here I am
Here I am
Just running 'round catching 'em
Whichever way they fall

Waiting on a Train

It's time that I was leaving
Should have left here long ago
You'd rather see me sorry
Than knowing what I know
I wish it was asleep instead
Of hanging here up above my head
I'm crying
In the wintertime, woman

Get all my shit together
Try for another breath
Lonely living sorrow
Holding on like death
From the play of lights below
Is that church bells ringing or the whistle blowing?
I don't care
I'm gone
Shooting up and down the tracks

Morning comes
Cold chills and shakes
Just reminding me of my mistake
Well, alright
Now get your smell off of me, mama

It's time that I was leaving
I left here long ago
You'd rather see me sorry
Than knowing what I know
Wish it was asleep instead
Of hanging here up above my head
Late, late in the midnight crawling
Just waiting on a train

Day and Night

Early morning I don't mind
That's when I find you
Find you under orange skies
I'm gonna try and shine
Blue drowning days
Thought I might go crazy
Blue lonesome nights away

Early evening I don't mind
That's when I find you
Find you under orange skies
Making me try and shine
Blue drowning days
Thought I was insane
Blue lonesome nights away

Praying Ground

Not feeling any pain
But I know that it's real
Never see the color of the day
In the darkness I kneel

Praying for sleep
Praying that it will come easy
But there's something else
I see it miles away

Don't know what time of year it is
I can't remember the fall
Yet all my strange and simple games
Play out on top of a wall

Praying for sleep
Praying for something so easy
If only the moon
Would have left me alone

Because of This

You take me back to a place where I cease to exist
To find in your kiss something I've missed
You burn away my disguise and galaxies fall
Because of this
Because of this

And it hurts
God knows that it does
And when it hurts sometimes
You're there to quiet my mind

Because of this
Because of this

You pry open my eyes
I resist but you do
And when I stumble and bleed
You give your body to me
Because of this
Because of this

You take me back to a place where I cease to exist
To find in your kiss something I've missed
You burn away my disguise and the heavens fall
Because of this
Because of this

And it hurts
God knows that it does
But when I stumble and bleed
You give your body to me
Because of this
Because of this

Field Songs

(2000–2001)

"Fuck!" . . . Silence . . . Three or four minutes of a repetitive pattern picked on an electric guitar and then . . . "Fuck!"

Standing under the hazy sun outside Duff McKagan's house in the Hollywood Hills, watching a row of falcons searching for prey hover motionless in the sky, and listening to guitarist Ben Shepherd alternately recording and cursing from inside the garage, I knew my living situation had seen a considerable upgrade. Thanks to my friend's kindness, I had gone from working construction in east L.A. and sleeping on a cot in someone's art studio to being "caretaker" of this hilltop home complete with recording studio, perched just above Mulholland Drive.

A year earlier I had re-signed with Sub Pop for one more record but had decided to give them two, an album of covers and one of originals. The problem was that I had spent most of the advance on the covers and didn't have much left over for what became "Field Songs," which is why my newfound dwelling place had extra importance: here I could record for free. I consider the finished album to be one of my best, and it contains some of my favorite songs: "Don't Forget Me," in which I flat-out took melody and phrasing from an Israeli folk song and was immediately busted for it by fans when it was released; "One Way Street," which has been a constant in my set lists since the day it came out; and "No

Easy Action," which I wrote after reading two stories in the newspaper one morning. The first covered an exhibition of photos from Ernest Shackleton's failed Antarctic expedition, and the second described the studio apartment of a Seattle man who caused a city bus to go off the side of the Aurora Avenue Bridge when he shot the driver and then himself. "Kimiko's Dream House" was a gift from my favorite singer, friend, and mentor Jeffrey Lee Pierce. He gave me the music and half the lyrics and said, "Finish it."

One Way Street

The stars and the moon
Aren't where they're supposed to be
But this strange electric light
It falls so close to me
Love, I come to ride
I am that seasick rolling wave
And you know that I am just trying to get down

Oh, the glorious sound
Oh, the one way street
But you can't get, can't get it down without crying

When I'm dressed in white send roses to me
I drink so much sour whiskey
I can't hardly see
And everywhere I've been there's a well that howls my name
From the one tiny sting to that vacant fame

Oh, the deafening roar
Remember, that's called a one way street
And you can't get, can't get it down without crying

Through the mysteries of sight, you can't get out
In the psychotropic light, you can't get out
Love, I come to ride
High on that seasick rolling wave
That's the way that I fall trying to get out

Oh, the glorious sound of the one way street
And you can't get, can't get it down without crying
Oh, the deafening roar
It's called a one way street . . .

No Easy Action

When all is done and turned to dust
And insects nest inside my bones, I see
I stagger in a daze outside my tent
No time for being alone to bleed

The hopeless singing of a round, that much we know to do
Before we go back underground
No easy action

Sparks fill the air some nights
Crows look for food behind my skin, they need
We try our best to dig it in
And keep the cold away, we see

That the sky is a vanishing place
And yet there's nothing to miss
No time to get out of the ice
No easy action

Although all else may turn to dust
And insects nest inside my bones, I see
I stagger in a daze to find what you meant
Where it's good to be alone to bleed

The hopeless singing of a round
Before that vanishing place
Before we're back underground
No easy action

Miracle

I promised you a miracle and it will be done
Upon this one last disappearing
Bells toll, new lands!
And I look up
Sometimes to see
This old black Mary reach down for me
I need someone for my plaything
I'm so lonesome in my playground
You, baby, go straight to my head
And make it seem like a miracle
And make it something beautiful
Something beautiful

Pill Hill Serenade

Taillights through silver rain
Somebody's excited to be going away
Spring like December on the corner now
Let the memory fade and I'll forget

Well, I hope she's not alone
Smiling everywhere she goes, so sweet
Then I remember she's a little older now
I'd let that fade, but I don't know how

And when the sun comes up dead
You get sick of it
It makes a howling in your head all the time

Springtime or December
Can't find cover now
Children may get excited
When the sun comes around
I'm gonna walk in silver rain
Look for mine the same
Walk for miles 'til the memory fades

And when the sun comes up dead
Makes it hard when you know
It's a story that gets told all the time

Don't Forget Me

Cool water divined
Now I'm thirstier with nowhere to go
And what else do we find
But sorrow and misery untold?
I know you got somebody new, much better than me
When that chain starts to swing, keep in mind one thing
Don't forget me, dear

And when you're lost, I feel it too
Woman, make life sweet
Because of what you do
All my world is you

Now we know it's not easy
Don't believe them when they say I'm not right
Don't put a hex on me, baby
Because I don't know what's wrong or right
I know that there's somebody new, much better than me
But because my love is true, all my best to you
Don't forget me, dear

And when you're alone, please take care
Don't go walking after dark
Shine a light behind the stairs
Remember what might be in there

Cool water divined
Now I'm thirstier with nowhere to go
It's sorrow that we find
I'm thirstier with nowhere to go
I know that there's somebody new, much better than me
When that chain starts to swing, keep in mind one thing
Don't forget me, dear
Because my love is true, I give my best to you
Don't forget me, dear

Kimiko's Dream House

It's a matter of time
We always get lost
Without going very far
It's a matter of time

Like I told you before
Things are alright
If I fall to the floor
It's for closing my eyes

I came to this place so tired at first
Kimiko's dream house
So many things the girl's known before
Kimiko's dream house
And so many things that I've known before

To make matters worse
The trains are on time
But we're lost in the station
Still lost in our minds

Thrown into reverse, we kicked and cursed
Kimiko's dream house
So many things the girl's known before
Kimiko's dream house
So many things that I've known before

It's swallowing us, but dream we must
Kimiko's dream house
So many things the girl's known before
Kimiko's dream house
So many things that I've known before

And all the girls have known me for

Resurrection Song

Day, end of day
Each hanging spiral
Where is the shore
From this deep blue silence?
Up to the heavens that you daydream
Remembering the sun and the deep green ivy
I know that sleepwalking too
And trying to be free
Of all this damage in my eyes
Making confusion in my mind
When I hear a resurrection song
It lays me down when I'm fading
When I can't go home because they hate me
To sing that resurrection song

Day, end of day
Each hanging spiral
What do you make
Of this deep blue silence?
Nod at the engine driver
He's grown to be a deep-sea diver
And the street has got no end
Better keep your heart strong, little friend
Thought I heard a resurrection song
Thought I heard a resurrection song

Field Song

Let's walk down to the water
There's hyacinth in bloom
I'll spend my days loving you
I left these fields because I never knew
To be a horse
To be a train
I wouldn't have the heart
Next to the tracks you find an apple cart
Maybe we'll stay at home and be together
No more to move alone
Together, no more to move alone
See the water, mixed with light
For you I've been shaken
Regarding the fields, humbly mistaken

Low

Love with my will
Love just what I can
Blood, that's all there is
In times of trial and loneliness
Too dark for finding my ground
And the trees shiver and sway
Have you ever seen something go down
To keep in mind all of your days?
Lord, you know where I've been
And you know why I came
Look, I'm all done in
Pray you don't send me back again
Tell her I wanted to say goodbye
Before the light was dead and gone
Tell her I didn't want to lie
And left here well enough alone

Lord, you know where I've been
And only you know why I came
Blood, that's all there is
Pray you don't send me back again
If I stayed away too long
And many times I lost my way
You ever been skeleton low?
Have you ever heard somebody say
Baby, baby, don't you know about love?

She Done Too Much

Got so sad the day she done too much
And though I had the same
She done too much
And it's a bad, bad feeling that you get
When you get so lonely

Nothing to talk about as another summer dies
And not a thing in this world to do
Except be alone in it

Fix

Fix
It's true
It keeps on raining, baby
So crystalline
In my head
Gonna watch from the balcony
Sing backwards and weep
Fix
It's true
It keeps raining, baby
Needs no explaining, baby
Gonna drive that Terraplane across a frozen ocean
We've always been together and it's good
Love will be what's hidden in every single fragment
I look and then I find a flower born from you
And I am joined with you
And adorned with you
Fix
It's true
It's gonna keep raining, baby
And it's you that I'm missing
When I come up missing
When I'm torn from you
Want to be reborn in you
So crystalline and bright
Fix
It's true
Keeps on raining, baby
Keeps on raining, baby
Drive that Terraplane down into the ocean
Always been together and it's good
Got no need for shelter
Everything's forgotten

All is forgiven and understood
A flower born from you
Reborn in you
And adorned with you
When I am joined with you
Fix
It's true
Keeps on raining, baby
Keeps on raining, baby

Houston Publishing Demos

(2002)

MY SOCKS were soaked with blood and my feet covered in huge open blisters, and I sat in discomfort on the blazing hot sidewalk trying to let them breathe for a minute. I had come down to Houston at a time of intense heat and extremely high humidity wearing an old pair of engineer boots a size and a half too big and with no money to buy new ones. I felt something sting my wrist and looked down just in time to see a frighteningly huge, solid black flying insect take wing after biting me and had to laugh at this comedy of errors. Things were not going great. I had also come down to Houston with only the barest of a bone-ragged collection of songs to fulfill a publishing contract I had signed with an old friend, producer and label head Randall Jamail, a talented man who took no shit from anyone and who would not have been pleased if he knew the honest state of my unprepared and unraveling songcraft, such as it was. For the better part of a week, I would walk around the parking lot outside the studio writing lyrics to a song that the band was inside recording and then would sit down on a bench with an acoustic guitar and write another one while they were doing overdubs on the last. Then I would show them the next song and, while they started to arrange it, would head outside again. At night I stayed awake in my room at a Holiday Inn off the freeway, coming up with songs for the next day and listening to the constant roar of traffic. Despite the haphazard, stumble-bum way the writing was done, Randall did a stunning production job and in time I came to realize that instead of a bunch of demos, he had actually shaped a unique record that stood on its own merit. Among the tunes that have stayed in my mind: "When It's in You," which is an early version of "Methamphetamine Blues" and has a sort of mild psychedelic vibe instead of the more strident industrial sound of the later version; "Grey Goes Black," a minimal miniature reflecting my numbness over events on 9/11; and "Way to Tomorrow," a song I wrote and recorded my last night in town upon receiving the devastating news that Layne Staley had died.

No Cross

No cross to carry
No cause to cry
We'll walk streets of gold in time
And when those shadows crawl in, run go get the priest
'Cause I won't miss a thing but you, my little freak

The million-dollar arms
And real blue heartache kids
Stroll to rock and roll dead slow
Put on their coats and go

All these empty arms ain't got nothing to do
But play some rock and roll dead slow
Put on my coat and go

No cross to carry
No grinding wheel to ride
No cross to carry
And no nails to drive

Two Horses

I check out when the dance is done
The world takes an overdose
I feed on the Easter flower
And search for that starry crown
I can't help it

I trip on the teeth and feathers
Outside the factory
My horses click their hooves together
And caravan down through the desert
I can't help it
I can't help it

I check out when the dance is done
Seen all I was meant to see
Blind men walking the high wire
Above an Eden of magnolia trees
I can't help it
I can't help it

I trip on the teeth and feathers
Outside the factory
My horses asking one another
Why have I led them to black water?
I can't help it
I can't help it
I can't help it

When It's in You (Methamphetamine Blues)

When it's in you
You won't wanna leave this living so soon
When it's in you
Now it's brand new
The days roll on like sugar, so sweet
When it's in you

The scarecrow stands at the top of the stairs
And I shoot
Let the radio play methamphetamine blues
Until I lose

Now that it's in you

When it's in you
You won't wanna leave this living so soon
When it's in you
Everything brand new
The days roll on like sugar, so sweet
Everything brand new

The scarecrow stands at the top of the stairs
And I shoot
Let the radio play methamphetamine blues
Until I lose

Now that it's in you
Now that it's in you

High Life

That strange little bird makes a pennywhistle sound
And I'm gonna live the high life
The very same thing all the fortunate have found
The world on a string
The high life

Black light, black heat
Who can resist?
It flows through time
It slows like this

That strange little bird makes a melancholy sound
But I'm gonna live the high life
It has been said that there's nothing so profound
As living it well, the high life
As living it well, the high life

I'll Go Where You Send Me

I'll go where you send me
I know better now
I'll go where you send me
I know better now
Never thought I'd see this beautiful thing
I know better now

Blue lights above me
I see your mercy now
Blue lights above me
I see your mercy now
And then to fall like nothing at all
Just a dream

I'll do what you ask me
I shall not want
I'll do what you ask me
And I shall not want
Your will be done, while mine has gone
Through every darkened place

I'll go where you send me
I'm ready now
I'll go where you send me
I'm ready now
Ready to fall like nothing at all
Just a dream

Grey Goes Black

Grey goes, goes black
Dead white and baby blue
In life there's a falling away
And a sad, sad coming
It rise from the burning tower
It walks in late and early hours
Yeah, yeah, yeah, yeah, yeah

The Primitives

Forget your family, son
The face on the clock, your foreign body
The ship is just a frame
Pinpoint eyes, seething decks, and pain

You wonder how it should be
You wonder how it should go
Then deny no loathsome thing
Hands beyond hands beyond oblivion swing

Forget your family, son
The face on the clock, your foreign body
The ship is just a frame
Pinpoint eyes, seething decks, and pain

Blind

Dirt by any other name
Wouldn't have a taste so sweet
Tell me, do I take the blame?
Or should I admit defeat?
Or go blind
Or go blind

Twisting, falling through the air
Will there be another day?
Gone so long you couldn't care
I hang my head down anyway
And go blind
And go blind

Dirt by any other name
Wouldn't have a taste so sweet
Tell me do I take the blame?
Or should I admit defeat?
Or go blind
Or go blind

Halcyon Daze

So these are the halcyon days
I'll do my suffering tomorrow
As a kid I knocked out windowpanes
And my perversities were limitless
Now I need somebody like you
Because I'm on my own and tired, it's true

Turn now, tipsy elephant
Do you mind me quietly riding you?
I don't have too far to go
Just a little longer
And I need somebody like you
Because I'm on my own and tired, it's true

So these are the halcyon days
I'll do my suffering tomorrow
I once knocked out windowpanes
And my cruelties were limitless
Now I need somebody like you
Because I'm on my own and tired, it's true
I need somebody like you
I'm on my own and tired, it's true

Nothing Much to Mention

Pack up that crystal chandelier
But leave some pink champagne on ice
There's nothing much to mention here
Should I dance around the room just like a child
To make it easy on your mind?
No long goodbyes

They say that love can make you weep
But make you very glad as well
Now all I think of love is sleep
I'd say I'm sorry, but what the hell
You've heard it all too many times
No long goodbyes

Pack up that crystal chandelier
But leave some pink champagne on ice
There's nothing much to mention here
Should I dance around the room just like a child
To make it easy on your mind?
No long goodbyes

A Suite for Dying Love

Can't write a suite for dying love
Can't find the trigger for the gun, oh yeah
So tired of holding up the sky
I'm twenty stories high, oh yeah
Why don't you give me one more kiss?
I'm coming down
I can't make nothing last
I'm coming down

I wanted to say goodbye before my train rolled out
Went walking away with a mouthful of rain
Gotta get back and see my friends again
Just a little ashamed they gotta see me this way
Galaxies should fall
I'm coming down
I can't make nothing last
Coming down

Way to Tomorrow

Carry that weight, but it's too heavy, lord
Walk that mile, but it's too far to go
Out in the wintertime
Lost, I can't get over
Can't find my way to tomorrow

There's driving rain, there's ice and there's snow
No place to rest, nothing to know
Look for some better times
But I can't get over
Can't find my way to tomorrow

Here Comes That Weird Chill/
Bubblegum

(2003–2004)

"MAN, THIS is becoming like a scene out of *A Beautiful Mind* . . . and not in a good way," said mix producer Rick Will, and I knew what he meant. I had been awake for days and nights, crazed from no sleep and illegal stimulants, and was sitting cross-legged on the studio floor with sheets of paper covered in handwritten lyrics, notes, and ideas strewn out around me in a ten-foot circle. While I had been out of my mind making records in the past, this was a new peak . . . or low, depending on one's perspective. For months I had been using the off-time from my gig as an auxiliary singer with Queens of the Stone Age to try and complete a record, but as usual, my own insanity would not allow it. When it was all said and done, I recorded enough for two records, with the title of the first coming from something Greg Dulli said while shuddering involuntarily in the suddenly cold wind walking to my car after a Twilight Singers recording session, and the title for *Bubblegum* coming from a lyric in the song "Bombed." Song favorites include "Skeletal History," where I tried to channel the free-form vocalisms of SST band Saccharine Trust to chart the skewed evolution of my own damaged species, "When Your Number Isn't Up," and "Strange Religion," a love song I wrote in a Tokyo hotel room. While many of the songs came from a place of dejection and ennui at the end of a tempestuous relationship, "Bombed" in particular came about when, after I had written and recorded it in just a few minutes, I put a microphone in front of Wendy Rae Fowler, my soon-to-be-ex-wife, and had her sing along while simultaneously hearing it for the first time. I loved the result as it reminded me of Royal Trux, a band I liked. When I insisted on using the first and only take of the song, it made her slightly unhappy, but to be fair, that was just one of many things I did that had that effect.

Methamphetamine Blues

Hit it

Wake up, wake up
Children, don't you hear me coming?
Get up, get up
Because I got to have the honey
And I don't wanna leave this heaven so soon

Rolling, children, keep on rolling
Rolling, children, keep on rolling
Keep the light turned low and the back door open
My love rain down like sugar so sweet
(I got what you want, so come and get it)
Yes, children, I will

John lawman rides with his uniform clean
Shine on his shoes
My radio plays methamphetamine blues
Until I lose
I'm rolling just to keep on rolling

Wake up children
Get right soul church, keep a lock on the kitchen
And do this for your daddy
(I'll do it daddy)
Keep your eyes wide open and my shotgun loaded
'Cause I don't wanna leave this heaven so soon

Rolling just to keep on rolling
Rolling just to keep on rolling
Rolling just to keep on rolling
My love rain down like sugar so sweet
(Got what you want, so come and get it)
Yes baby

John lawman rides with his uniform clean
Shine on his shoes
My radio plays methamphetamine blues
Until I lose

I'm rolling just to keep on rolling
I'm rolling just to keep on rolling
Rolling just to keep on rolling
I don't wanna leave this heaven so soon

Rolling just to keep on rolling
Rolling just to keep on rolling
Rolling just to keep on rolling

I don't wanna leave this heaven so soon

On the Steps of the Cathedral

Tired of being devilish
Sick of being wicked
Habitual and untrue
Another starting over
Although it isn't in me, I send regards to you
Standing on the steps
Steps of the cathedral
Watching summer fade
I was trying to get to somewhere
Trying to get just anywhere
But now I know it ain't my day

Message to Mine

Oh it's good, baby
To make me forget
Oh so good, baby
So good to make me forget
Forget myself again

I walk down the steps to the river
With my outfit, full set to deliver
In a minute it's done, nothing but time
On a pay telephone send a message to mine

Yeah, it's good
So good, baby
Because it makes me forget
Oh so good
So good, baby
Because it made me forget
Forget myself again

Upstairs, slower on my feet
I gotta get to the corner, and I know it's getting late
At the cold polar ice end of the line
If I don't wake up, send a message to mine

Oh so good
So good, baby
Because it makes me forget
Forget myself again

Seventeen steps down to the river
With my outfit full set to deliver
When the floodlights shine, blinding my eye
On a pay telephone I send a message to mine

Back down early in the morning
Same building, different story
Well, the room here is free and it's easy to find
The quicksilver veins send a message to mine

Yeah, so good
So good, baby
Because it makes me forget
Oh so good
So good, baby
Because it makes me forget
Forget myself again

Lexington Slow Down

It won't break my heart
Won't hope to die
If, before Lexington, I could slow down
They say a chariot's waiting when you get cut loose
Let the place start swinging when it's me on the noose

Mother, do you think that your children cry
Because they wanna shake your chain?
I walked miles today
One for every year of my life
In this stinking, fucking rain

Just to slow down
So I could slow down
So I could slow down

Work for me luck, just one last time
Spare me a chance, I've wasted mine
Shine on me, light
Don't you know I would
Reach for you there if only I could?
If I could slow down
If I could slow down
If I could slow down
Just slow down

I don't mind being stoned, they say jesus was
And I like being alone
And I can take living low
Forgive my being cruel if ever I was
Say a word for me too when I'm under the gun

It wouldn't break my heart
If I could slow down
Let the place start swinging
If there's a chariot waiting
It wouldn't break my heart
If I could slow down
Let the place start swinging
If there's a chariot waiting

It wouldn't break my heart

Skeletal History

An artery is not a vein
No history can tell
My skeleton won't tell
Why some, like moths, draw
To the surgeon's drill
And bloodshot hits to marrow
The snake's eaten through her clothes
And her charms have won me over
Da Gama breached this lofty reach
Balboa left his bones upon the beach
Left there to bleach
A rose breaks in my fingers
Pulling nickels through the stem too much has took a toll
Smoke crawls low along the ceilings
And all is quiet, but I keep listening
They come to kill me

Oh, she just left, you missed her
Go on home
The sex theater is closed
Crack mouth too dry to drink
At least the sand is cold
You wish the sea would drown the freeway
Instead, girls stare in dead-eyed wonder
They can't walk for falling soldiers
Used by cops
And fucked inside abandoned boardinghouses
Go on fast before the beast catches the bastard
Dragging a chain down down down
Who'll say it tell me?
No one else is here, c'mon
Nothing to believe is to be blessed, c'mon
The wolf's laying low, you said

Weathervanes and bones to be
Good or bad, the death of me
Just make it quietly
Oh, who knows my sister?
Can't anyone admit the fact that they infected her?
She said the sun was gonna burn and blister
My blood
Godspeed
God
Love her
Farewell, honey
Yeah
No mourning son'll move her
No hellbent amen or hallelujah
Prayers are for the dead left over
The breached never to reach that sandy beach
The poor baby girl's gone under
To each their own grave buried in
Underneath abandoned boardinghouses
Sidewalks and streets
Sidewalks and streets

Though my skeleton won't tell
Some can see
Why moths draw to surgeon's drills
And blood shots hit the marrow

Wish You Well

He wrote her name with a needle gun
In black and blue
Your eyes are stone, she said
Beautiful and dead
And I wish you well

I took a turn on this carousel
How long ago I never can tell
I never stopped to wonder

Maybe a morning
Maybe a thousand years
I only walk high wires
To tend an Eden,
Of magnolias dying

And though I'm coarse and primitive
I wish love, lord
I wish love could live
Forever

What I once saw burning bright as hell
Now here comes that weird chill
Don't stop to wonder

I threaded her name through the needle's eye
As it frayed
Tied the ends and stitched it up
Then hung my head down and wept
But I wish you well

Who will pray for the killer's sake?
I used to be so wide awake
Like certain mornings
That last a thousand hours

Though I'm coarse and primitive
I wish love, lord
I wish love could live forever
Once burning bright as hell
Now here comes that weird chill
But I wish you well
Your eyes are stone, she said
Truly beautiful and dead, I wish you well

I only ride on this carousel
I never really stop to wonder

Sleep with Me

With heavy head and harbor mined
The red sun claws at my bloodshot eye
The faithful have scattered
They're running away
Along for the ride went all of my shame
Now I need someone
Sleep with me, sleep with me
Dark night coming, won't you sleep with me?

These feral girls will suit me more
Than gloss from drugstore magazines
Your werewolf teeth flicker and gleam
You're someone who saw
The same way I see
At the turn of a century
Skip thin dimes on sheets of ice
I got my eyes on you
You got your eyes on me

The angels have scattered
Swearing to god
The albatross dives on the firing squad
And I need someone
Sleep with me, sleep with me
Dark night coming, won't you sleep with me?

Heavy head and asphalt lined
Gift horse pissed in my bloodshot eye
The dead dream on
The neon stare
The ambulance crawls
The siren I hear
And it finds me anywhere
The faithful have scattered
They're running away
Along for the ride went all of my shame
Because I need someone
You're looking at me
I got my eyes on you
The world is falling away
And it's a dark night

When Your Number Isn't Up

Did you call for the night porter?
You smell the blood running warm
I stay close to this frozen border
So close I can hit it with a stone

Now something crawls right up my spine
That I always got to follow
Turn out the lights
Don't see me drawn and hollow
Just blood running warm

No one needs to tell you that
There's no use for you here anymore
And where are your friends?
They've gone away
It's a different world, and they left you to this
To janitor the emptiness
So let's get it on

When the sun is finally going down
And you're overdue to follow
But you're still above the ground
What you've got coming
Is hard to swallow
Like blood running warm

Did you call for the night porter?
You smell the blood, blood running warm
Well I've been waiting at this frozen border
So close you could hit it with a stone

Hit the City

The dog descends through the promised land
Down kingdom come and the acid bath
I'm Babylon burned inside out
Nothing to kill it
I hit the city

In Maryanne I dug a hole
And watched her trip on my hollow soul
Then in the end
All that crawled was my skin
I couldn't kill it
I hit the city
I hit the city

The ghost arrives at his bitter end
To the promised land then the dog descends
I'm Babylon burned inside out
Nothing to kill it
I hit the city
I hit the city
I hit the city

Wedding Dress

Would you put on that long white gown
And burn like there's no more tomorrows?
Will you walk with me underground
And forgive all my sicknesses and my sorrows?
Will you be shamed if I shake like I'm dying
When I fall to my knees and I'm crying?
Will you visit me where my body rests?
Will you put on that long white dress?

The end could be soon
We better rent a room
So you can love me

Will you put on that long white dress
While I burn when there's no more tomorrows?
Will you remember me through the years I'll miss
And forget all the sadnesses and the sorrows?

We got buried in a fever
Now you love me

One Hundred Days

When the willow bends toward the end of day
And twilight falls again
To the funny sound that a blackbird makes
Twilight falls again
As no good reason remains
I'll do the same, thinking of you

One day a ship comes in
One day a ship comes in
And I can't say how or when
But I know somewhere a ship comes in every day

There is no morphine
I'm only sleeping
There is no crime to dreams like this
And if you could take something with you
It would be bright
Just like something good

From my fingertips
The cigarette throws ashes to the ground
I'd stop and talk to the girls who work this street
But I got business farther down
Like one long season of rain
I will remain, thinking of you

One day a ship comes in
From far away a ship comes in
One hundred days you wait for it
And you know somewhere a ship comes in every day

There is no morphine
I'm only sleeping
There is no crime to dreams like this
And if you could take something with you
It would be bright
Just like something good
One day a ship comes in
One hundred days you wait for it
Something bright
Something so good
Is it good?
Give me something good

Bombed

Love there are flowers hanging in the vine
So high you cannot see
Now my mind must go on holiday
Torn from its hook, a broken valentine

I see the smoke from a revolver
Will I get hit? I hardly care
When I'm bombed
I stretch like bubblegum
And look too long straight at the morning sun

Love there are flowers along the avenue
All things perfectly in place
I build a shrine
I set a monument
Because you're fire
Because you're a fire escape

Strange Religion

Can you stay here next to me?
We'll just keep driving
Because of you I see a light
The Buick's a century
A '73 like you
Some strange religion

I get my hands on some money, mama
And it's shot in a night
Stared down the past and just scarred my eyes
Now I know there's no easy ride
She's been the kind who would take it in stride
Some jack of diamonds kicked her heart around
Did they know they were walking on holy ground?

I almost called it a day so many times
Didn't know what it felt like to be alive
Until you been a friend to me
Like nobody else could be

Keep my hands on the wheel now, mama
I'm gonna honestly try
She looked past the scars and the burned-out eyes
And could see I'm no easy ride
She's just the kind who might get you to buy
Some strange religion

These jacks of diamonds kicked her heart around
Should have known they were walking on holy ground
And this life might eventually just be the end of me
And I'll still be with you

Can you get in here next to me?
I just keep driving
Because of you I've been alive
And this Buick's a century
A '73 like you
Some strange religion
The Buick's a century
'73 like you
Some strange religion

Sideways in Reverse

On a dead high wire where I make a connection
Never knowing my shepherd
Never knowing my witness
C'mon now honey, you're so sick and pretty
C'mon now sugar, 'cause you know it ain't easy

Bang bang bang
Let me shoot it all over
(Going down people, give me your love)
You're another mistake
You're a sign of disaster
(Going down people, give me your love)
Gonna shake shake shake
As a matter of course
(Going down, going down, people, give me your love)
It bites like a bitch
And it kicks like a horse
(Going down, going down, people, give me your love)

Ain't you glad, ain't you glad, ain't you glad, little sister
Sideways in reverse, I don't know any better
You gotta keep it running clean
Keep on fixing the machine
Keep it running clean
Keep on fixing the machine

Come to Me

Come to me
Light on my shoulder
Come to me
Burn your starry crown
My dark angel
I've tried, I can't get over
Just when I think I'm climbing
I'm really so far down

Time takes a while
To break you
And now only fire can wake you

Weeping willow
I'm coughing up my heart
Has god seen my shadow
And kept us apart?

Through my mind's every riot or revelation
You've just now gone
As I arrive at every station

Oh, come to me
Either early or late
I've learned this by habit
Now I know how to wait

Come to me
Come to me

Like Little Willie John

There was nothing I could do

Where's Willie John?
Dead so long
Born to fall
Nothing at all
Who's gonna grieve when you're gone?
I once believed I wouldn't bleed

I seen all these good-looking women
While I'm getting off the plane
And remember where my baby is
Start thinking 'bout my baby

All she ever knew was trouble
And for much I was to blame
But when I heard the news that night
I went down like a satellite
And when my world stood still that night
I dropped like a satellite

She never knew how much I loved her
She never knew how much I cared
I thought I'd get back to my special one
I thought I'd get on a lucky run
I said I'd get back to my special one
I said I'd get on a lucky run
Goddamn

Where's Willie John?
Dead so long
Born to fall
Like nothing at all
Now who's gonna grieve when you're gone?
I once believed I'd never bleed

But, lord, I'm all alone tonight
Don't the sun love its satellite?
Lord, I'm all alone tonight
Don't the sun love its satellite?
I don't know

I seen all these good-looking women
And remember where my baby is
Start thinking 'bout my baby
Remember where my baby is
Start me thinking 'bout my baby
Where's my baby?

Can't Come Down

I don't give a damn for money
Never did I give a damn for gold
Tell me, little doll
Talk some sweet nothings
The river runs deep and cold

I don't know why, but it keeps running
I don't know why I can't come down

Moses, he stood on a mountain
The devil made it thunder and rain
Girl, I ain't afraid of temptation
No, I ain't afraid of some pain

Watch a little doll
She just come running
Running straight away
Bring it to me, I got sweet nothing
And only myself to blame
I don't know why I just keep running
I don't know why I can't come down

Walk
Don't you walk on me
Don't you step
Don't you step on me
Don't you walk
Don't walk on me
Don't you step on me

Ain't got a thing for money
Got no jones for gold
All I got today is some sweet nothing
Nothing to take away
Don't know why I just keep running
Don't know why I can't come down

Morning Glory Wine

The first time I loved was electrocution
Then I fell out on the down
Blind with injection

Strawberry
The way you come naked
Out here you're alone
These streets get very cold, you should know
Yeah, and don't I know

Are we gonna be judged?
Judged on these lonely deeds?
Are we gonna cry?
Yeah
Are we gonna freeze?

Morning glory wine
Good people don't drink it
So long alone not thinking
Please

How you thrill me, love
How you kill me, love
Like electrocution

Monday's own has lost her luck
Tuesday shakes and pleads
Friday comes and calls your bluff
Sunday's on her knees
That's how you'd do me, love
If you knew me, love
But there ain't no one to turn to
It's hard when you're on your own
And you lost your way home

Morning glory wine
Good people don't drink it
So long on my own not thinking
Please
That's how you do me, love
That's how you do me, love
Like electrocution
Like electrocution

Morning glory wine
Good people don't drink it
Its hard when you're on your own
And you lost your way home
And there ain't nobody, baby
Nobody to turn to

Is there somebody?
Somebody to turn to
I'll be somebody, baby
Someone to turn to
I wanna get high
On morning glory wine
Get me high
When there ain't nobody, baby
I'll be someone to turn to

I'll be somebody to turn to

Head

So sad, the girl I had
Lost her head and it went bad
Blue, her two eyes they were dead
The mirror mine would see, she said

One of these mornings
I don't know her
One of these mornings
I think I owe her

Head
Oh yeah

Once she signed a piece of my mind
In gutter scenes and gasoline
A porno pony she did ride
Forsaken long lost limousine

I hear her talking
I like to hear her talking
See her walking
I like to watch
Watch her come walking

Head
Oh yeah

She lost it, and man, did it get bad
Her lazy eyes were dead
The mirror mine would see, she said

Once she drew a picture
Stuck it in my pocket
Once I went to reach her
Once she let me rock it

Head
Oh yeah
Head
Oh yeah

See her walking
I like to watch
Watch her come walking

Head

Driving Death Valley Blues

Well, I'm so tired of driving, but here comes the highway
Don't wanna go cold turkey
Ride with me, jesus, so high on the mainline
It's the last time I'll drive Death Valley

Remember, her kiss is like kerosene
The rest of her only a memory
Don't feel so bad 'cause you made me
A picture so clear
Picture so clear that it's crystalline

Better run to the doctor
Girl, run to the medicine
Don't wanna go cold turkey
I'll be your Napoleon Be your crippled Alexander
But I don't wanna go up the country

Shame there's nothing to hang it on
Except for this wreck that you made of me
A blackbird singing a mourning song
Sing along
Sing to the end of the century

Well, I can't stand the thought of many more miles
But I don't wanna go cold turkey
Here comes the highway
Can't you see what it made me
It's the last time I'll drive Death Valley

Remember, her kisses are kerosene
The exile lives in her memory
A scarecrow singing a mourning song
Sing along
Sing to the end of the century

Are you still with me, jesus, so high on the mainline?
Don't make me go up the country
Girl, better run better run for the medicine
Don't let me go cold turkey

Out of Nowhere

As it begins, so too it ends
Crawls to a stop and starts again
Those highlights you forced to shine
Show me my way through wilderness
And someday far from here I'll send a kiss
Out of nowhere

At times, you see a ghost down on the street
It walks the hallway knocking door to door
Where are you from night 'til nine a.m.?
Only a dark skinned jesus knows
Why suddenly your room is turning cold
Cold as nowhere

And as it ends, so it begins
Crawls to a stop and starts again
Those highlights you made are mine
Show me my way through wilderness
To someone who's blind I'll send a kiss
Out of nowhere

Soulsavers

(2004–2009)

CRAWLING ALONG through a brutal, funereal Los Angeles rush hour traffic jam, already an hour late for a recording session with British electronica act Soulsavers, scrolling down the car radio dial, I came across a strange Christian station and heard an elderly woman's faraway, ghostlike voice speaking with fervor about an old-fashioned tent revival. Something in the sound and weird power of her tone sent an electric jolt through my hands, and I barely avoided hitting a truck in front of me, slamming on the brakes at the last second. At that moment it became clear that the lyrics I had for this tune I was heading in to record were uninspired. After an hour more in the car and another ten smoldering dog-ends added to the overflowing coffee cup that functioned as an ashtray, I arrived at the studio with an entirely new singing part and revised words to go with it for "Revival." The genesis for this collaboration began in 2004 with a chance meeting backstage at the legendary Leadmill venue in Sheffield, England, where Soulsaver Rich Machin stirred my interest by handing me a disc of stark and moody instrumentals and asking if I'd sing on them, beginning an association that would last several years and lead to two records, *It's Not How Far You Fall, It's the Way You Land* and *Broken*.

Revival

Is there gonna be a revival tonight?
Oh, I wanna see a revival
Yeah
Gonna be a revival tonight
Lord, let there be a revival
Yeah
Forgive what I have done
It means my soul's survival
Oh oh oh
I need you so it's sin
To put an end to my suffering
Oh oh oh
Why am I so blind with my eyes wide open?
Trying to get my hands clean in dirty water

I wanna see a revival tonight
Lord, let there be a revival
Yeah
I need to see a revival tonight
Oh, I wanna see a revival
Oh oh oh
Why am I so blind with my eyes wide open?
Now I need someone
Let this dark night be done
Oh oh oh
I need you so it's sin
Put an end to my suffering
I wanna see a revival tonight
Lord, there needs to be a revival

Ghosts of You and Me

Goodbye Mary
Sweet mother mine
Grey as sky, gunmetal eyes
Beneath the needle tree
The ghosts of you and me
They sang the saddest song
Just one last breath and gone

Some say this highway seven
Is a long and lonesome road
Don't ask me, little Rosa
What direction I am gone
I used to love
And take the southern special
Winter, summer, rise or fall
Now I ride the national

If I had a black cat bone
Then I would not be alone
Julie, darling, dig my grave
The cemetery is my home

Goodbye Mary
Sweet mother mine
Grey as sky, gunmetal eyes
Under a needle tree
The ghosts of you and me
They sang the saddest song
Just one last breath and gone

I used to love
And take the southern special
Winter, summer, rise or fall
Now I take the national
Some say this highway seven
Is a long and lonesome road
Don't ask me, little Rosa, what direction, I don't know

If I had a black cat bone
Then I would not be alone
If I had a black cat bone
Then I would not be alone

Paper Money

Heaven so far away
Heaven just a taste
Heaven so far away

Cherry cherry cherry
Cherry cherry cherry
Cherry cherry cherry, baby
Heaven so far away

Cherry on your lips
Heaven so far away

Tell me baby
Who's your daddy?
He can't love like me
I keep a-burning baby
Like paper money
I give to you easy

I keep a-burning baby
The cherry on your lips
Is heaven so far away

Don't you ever leave me, baby
I believe that you can save me
Heaven just a taste
Heaven so far away
You wanna get me high
You can do it, baby
Gonna get me high
Keep a-burning baby
You're gonna get me high
I'm like paper money
Girl, who's your daddy?
He can't love like
He can't love like me

I keep burning, baby
I'm paper money
Girl, you know your daddy
He can't love like me
Can't love you, baby
He can't love like me
I keep a-burning baby
I'm like paper money
I keep a-burning baby
Heaven so far away

Jesus of Nothing

Last go-round
Seems like my trial's nearly ended
I been locked up
Going out of my head

The last go-round
Seems like my trial's nearly over
Been locked up
Going out of my mind

Jesus of nothing
Judas to touch us
On my way
Going out of my head
Last go-round
My trial's nearly ended

What's blocking out the sun
And turned the ocean over?
Sinner, where to run?
I've run so far already
A last go-round
To the end of my mind

Jesus of nothing
Judas to touch us
Last go-round
On my way
Going out of my head

Last go-round
My trial's nearly ended
It's my last go-round
My trial's nearly over
I'm on my way
Going out of my head

Death Bells

Death bells are ringing, lord
Ringing in my ears
Death bells keep ringing, ringing
Baby, can't you hear?

Death bells are ringing, lord
Ringing in my ears
Death bells keep ringing, ringing
Baby, can't you hear?

No one to crawl a thousand hours
No one at all to grow my graveyard flower
And this useless drift is a drag
No medicine and no remedies
And it may be my blood is cursed
But I'm breathing under my brother's dirt

Angels are singing, lord
Singing in my ears
Angels keep singing, singing
Baby, can't you hear?

Unbalanced Pieces

The sky is red
Clouds are grey
And copper moon
Some day I'll tell you
The threats are veiled, snow-blind at first
Unfurl the sails
For heavens blue
Or dark uncertain waters

Gone
Now carry on through violent seasons
I call you mother, mother, mother, in vain
Absent chain
The twilight's bleeding
And the playing board has two unbalanced pieces

No word is said
Castle grey and Sunday soon
Someday I'll kill you
The raining sheets batter the ground
Unroll the streets
And walk along on high uncertain wires

Gone
Now carry on through seasick seasons
I'm crawling mother, mother, mother, in vain
Absent frame
The twilights kneeling
And the chessboard still has two unbalanced pieces

All the Way Down

Warm summer breeze
Seems to whisper your name
Stoned in the sunlight
I know it's a shame

Fading away in the crystalline dawn
Upon six white horses the carriage is drawn

All the way down
Seems like I can't come up no more
Won't be happy again

Cold morning stars
Seem to shimmer unknown
The tide takes you under
You're rolling alone

Follow the tune that the siren would sing
Follow the moon, do you find anything?

All the way down
Pardon me for praying hard
For crying out loud

Warm summer breeze
Seems to whisper your name
Stoned in the sunlight
I know it's a shame

Drifting away in the crystalline dawn
Upon six white horses the carriage is drawn

All the way down
Seems like I can't come up no more
Won't be happy again
All the way down

Shadows Fall

I see circles of gold
In spite of my eyes
When darkness falls from above
Stay under me, my love

I see circles of gold
Fading to black
Until the heavens have died
You'll be the thorn in my side

Come so coldly awake where the light wouldn't go
Come only to drift downward slow

In the dying light
Is a dream beyond time
One as impossible
As it is beautiful

Now the ghost in the mirror
Twists this way and that
Setting the thread to fray
In such a solitary way

And the archangel sighs
Feeding his blues
Still I am loath to gather
All of these bones together

Come so coldly awake where the light wouldn't go
Come only to drift downward slow
On the way to the gate
Walk a merciful mile
While lying in wait, a serpent coils

Here's where the bent and the wretched were born
Here's where the path was erased in the storm

I see circles of gold
Burned off the sun
When shadows fall from above
Stay close to me, my love

Can't Catch the Train

Wait, wait
The race has been numbered
So soon to go
Where the horses have gone
Lay down your head
Like a baby to slumber
Can't make it home anymore
Oh no
Can't catch the train

With sorrows to suffer unknown
Drawing the stars to a close

As sure as the shovel
Is blind, deaf, and digging
One day you're hung
At the end of the rope
Hat in your hand
At the station just begging
Don't have the fare anymore
Oh no
Can't catch the train

Calling from beyond the pale
Shipwrecked, the dancers will crawl

Sing, sing
For a new day appearing
Give us one more
For the memories you lost
Sing for the night
And how quickly it's nearing
Can't make it home anymore
Oh no
Can't catch the train

Pharaoh's Chariot

To thank you, jealous heart
I put you in the ground
The driver rides the rain
The trumpeter, he sounds
As blood is to the root, is silver to the crown
Take it as you may
My love has gone away

Then it all comes to nothing
Then it all comes to nothing

To break you, jealous heart
I build to tear it down
The timber from the walls
The makeup from the clown
And dirt is to the grave as water to the drowned
So long to my slave
My wheel's beneath the waves

Then it all comes to nothing
Then it all comes to nothing

Rolling Sky

Is that somebody calling
Perhaps my love so long forgotten?
Now the snake wrapped around my arm
Has bared its teeth
Has done its harm

Rain
Rolling sky
Sing a broken lullaby
And the rose, paint it red
Because my love
It isn't dead
Isn't dead

Who has left the water running?
In suicidal waves it's coming
This sleepwalking prayer of mine
Is locked away
Has done its time

Dry
The weeping eye
Send a crippled valentine
Because the noise in my head
Says my love
It isn't dead
Isn't dead

Has God Seen My Shadow?

THESE ARE previously unreleased songs from various different time frames and recording sessions that were collected for an anthology released in 2013.

"To Valencia Courthouse" was literally written in the back seat of a car while on my way to a court appearance in Valencia, California, and the recording of "Sympathy" features the voice of one of my favorite singers, the incomparable Natasha Shneider. "Dream Lullabye" was my response to a challenge from close friend and fellow gutter twin Greg Dulli to write an unabashedly pretty song, and Dylan Carlson is the "D" from "Blues for D," a song about absent friends, life on Seattle's First Hill, and the hard times we shared there. "Leaving New River Blues" was recorded with a four-track machine in a hotel room on the Gold Coast of Australia and on the surface is about the disintegration of my brief, ill-fated first marriage, but like most of my songs is really just about myself.

Dream Lullabye

On such a quiet night
The setting sun drops through the clouds
And this is everything I need
I hear you whisper in the trees
Now I got a dream of my own
I'm alone and I am free
Yesterday don't matter no more
And a paper boat drifts from the shore
Drifts like my dreaming
Weeping willow, I ain't weeping no more
I got a dream, I got a dream
Now I got a dream of my own
No crying for what's been lost
Yesterday don't matter no more
Can't stop my dreaming
Can't stop my dreaming
Can't stop dreaming no more

Leaving New River Blues

I had to leave New River
After being married there
Couldn't get back home again
So long I ceased to care
I start to fiend and shake
Until heaven was dry

Went on to old Charleston,
Found more trouble there
Couldn't give up on this gambling
And lost far more than my fair share
Oh, and heaven was dry

The first thing that you learn now, love
As you ride a broken pony
You learn to love the dirt now, love
You love what can't be loved enough
If you fiend like some do
Then heaven is dry

When heaven is dry, baby
You exist for what you need
When the hurting starts for real now, baby
You'd crawl from Dallas to New Orleans
If you need like some do
Then heaven is dry
Oh, heaven is dry

Leaving New River blues

Sympathy

Remember to have sympathy
I'm lying on the floor
And what I use to murder me
Takes longer than before

And everything's a drag without you here
These times when I'm not seeing things too clear
I've scattered thoughts and chased the light away
But I am so in need of you today

I realize what calls my eyes to close
Is still or otherwise
I'd follow where the water falls
Until it disappears

I've been as poor as any man can be
Come chase this cloud that's fallen over me
Do you still love the games that I love, dear
There's no one else to play them with me here

Have sympathy
Have sympathy

To Valencia Courthouse

Good thing, have you gone away
Leaving those tears to dry?
All good things got to go that way
Though I can't say why
But the rippling breeze, magic mountains and all
Make for a beautiful day

You can open up the iron gates
You can give my mind a change of mood
And lately I have learned some things
From being distracted by you
Another go around the block
Another telephone call

Gone is the satellite, the one true believer
Gone is my broken ballerina
Remember the times you were taken over
Bathed in a radiant lover's light
Until another day

Good thing, have you gone away
Leaving those tears to dry?
Again, I know it goes that way
Though I can't say why
And I can't stand up to fall
And I don't need nothing at all
Oh, it's a beautiful day

A Song While Waiting

The moon touches spring
Lift your hands and fall through the air
I don't know what I'd bring
Short of drifting away somewhere
I know about waiting

It's cold, hold on to me
And belong to me wherever I go
The one who wears your rosary
I can't help myself, it's been too long already

What do they know about waiting?
Until the last fallen leaves have stopped breathing

The moon looks for spring
Lift your hands and fall through the air
I don't know what I'd bring
Short of drifting away somewhere
But I know about waiting

It's cold, hold on to me
And belong to me wherever I go
The one who wears your rosary
I can't help myself, it's been too long already

What do they know about waiting?
Until the last fallen leaves have stopped bleeding

Blues for D

In the coldest time of year
The strangest gift has found me here
Where boardinghouses used to be
Now these torn shades are all I see

From a window up above
I hear old voices begin cascading
I stop awhile and then
The medicine is already fading
If not for you, I'd rather go
To the harbor down below
To all my friends I'll always miss
I don't have time for one more kiss

All along the road
The trees and the wind seem to be weaving
And off the avenue
The morning is already leaving
It's time I quit and did the same
Gone from the terrace down to St. James
To take a look at what I've known
But did not know how to tell you so
To all my friends I'll always miss
Don't have time for one more kiss

No Contestar

Lay down your head in the shifting light
When it starts to fade
When it starts to fade

My mind plays a trick of a lethal kind
Drifting away
Drifting away

Now I concede I may have lived too long
Close to the bone
Close to the bone

When there's no knock upon the door
You'll know it's me
When your phone doesn't ring

And now as the day begins to die
You can call me
But when you call me
There's no reply

Blues Funeral
(2012)

IT WAS 6 a.m. on a ranch in Simi Valley, California, and I was up on a forklift, chain-smoking cigarettes while painting the ceiling of a barn converted into a gymnasium for a weight-loss reality television show. I had been on the job as a scenic painter for over a year and enjoyed the physical and always changing nature of building sets on various TV programs: *Biggest Loser, Judge Judy, Big Brother* (from which I was shitcanned for using the wrong color of paint on a bedroom inside the house), and so on.

In the aftermath of a near-death experience, music no longer had any effect on me. I had seen no white lights or tunnels to heaven but instead just woke up as if from sleep after five days in ICU to find a hollow tube the size of an extra thick pencil jammed halfway up my dick and a breathing apparatus down my throat. It was as if I'd been drained of all feeling and had zero desire to even listen to music, much less sing or write it. So I had found other means of making a living.

At some point in between jobs I had traveled back to my hometown in Washington State to visit family, and while playing pool one night with two of my nephews, the conversation turned to their interests.

"Uncle Mark, do you play video games?" Remembering that a few weeks earlier my manager had left a message with an offer to do the initial trailer tune for the release of a highly touted new shooter called *Rage*, I replied that I thought someone had asked me to do the music for one. Urged on by my sister's teenage sons, I somewhat half-heartedly called back and agreed to take on the task.

Back in Los Angeles, though, the process of writing and recording this song (entitled "Burning Jacob's Ladder") led to a sudden and unexpected reawakening of my love for music, and once it was completed, producer Alain Johannes and I continued recording, and the resulting collection of songs became my most successful record, *Blues Funeral*. If forced to choose only one of my albums to play live, this would be it. "The Gravedigger's Song" was something I had originally tried to use on someone else's recording, but it didn't make sense until a drumbeat lifted from an Adam Ant song proved to be its missing component, and "Riot in My House" was inspired, like many of my tunes through the years, by the music of Swedish band The Leather Nun. Danish director Nicolas Winding Refn's *Pusher* trilogy was the stimulus behind the lyrics for "Ode to Sad Disco," and its music was taken in part from the *Pusher II* soundtrack. *Blues Funeral*'s title is an homage to the great T. S. McPhee's band The Groundhogs, and its overall sound is reflective of my Krautrock listening habit, in particular an affection for Neu!, Cluster, Harmonia, and especially Kraftwerk.

The Gravedigger's Song

With piranha teeth
I've been dreaming of you
And the taste of your love, so sweet
Honest, it's true

Through my heart flows sleep
And a dog-heavy rain
Where the gravedigger's song is sung
You've been torturing me

Tout est noir, mon amour
Tout est blanc
Je t'aime, mon amour
Comme j'aime la nuit

Love, is the medicine good?
Is the crow flying eight miles high
Over wire and wood?

Shovel down six feet
With a head-heavy pain
The magnolia blooms so sweet
And it fades just the same

To the stars, my love
To the sea
To the wheels, my love
'Til they roll all over me

Oh love, I've been thinking of you
With razor wire teeth so sharp
Honest, it's true

In my blood flows sleep
And a dog-heavy rain
The magnolia blooms so sweet
Only torturing me

To the stars, my love
To the sea
To the wheels, my love
'Til they roll all over me

Bleeding Muddy Water

Lord, now the rain done come
Lord, now the rain done come

Muddy water
Rising up
You know I feel you
In my iron lung
Muddy water
Celestial flood
You know I feel you
In my iron lung

I feel you
Feel you
In my iron lung
Muddy water
Lord now the rain done come

Oh baby don't it feel so bad?
Oh baby, baby don't it feel so bad?
Oh baby, baby don't it feel so bad?
Muddy water
Drowning in the rain
Now the rain done come

Muddy water
Pillar to post
How do I bleed you?
Just like a ghost
Muddy water
Heaven's son
You are the bullet
You are the gun

You're the bullet
Bullet
Bullet and the gun
Muddy water
You're heaven's son

Oh baby don't it feel so bad?
Oh baby, baby don't it feel so bad?
Oh baby, baby don't it feel so bad?
Muddy water
Drowning in the rain
Now the rain done come

Muddy water
Be my grave
You are the master
I've been the slave
Muddy water
Come rising up
You know I feel you
In my iron lung

I feel you
Feel you
In my iron lung
Muddy water
Lord, now the rain done come

Oh baby don't it feel so bad?
Oh baby, baby don't it feel so bad?
Oh baby, baby don't it feel so bad?
Muddy water
Drowning in the rain
Now the rain done come
Muddy water
Drowning in the rain
Now the rain done come

Gray Goes Black

Don't you turn off my radio
Please don't turn off my radio
Not with the rope still swinging
While eternity's mouth is singing

So insect, I'm in amber
Days go by, please don't forget
Uneven, so enamored
Days go by, remember that

Gray goes black

Can't you hear my radio?
Don't you hear my radio?
Not with the beast still sleeping
While eternity's eyes are weeping

So insect, I'm in amber
Days go by, please don't forget
Uneven, so enamored
Days go by, remember that

Gray goes black

Into the blood we sink and burn
Gray goes black
Into the blood we sink and burn
Gray goes black

St. Louis Elegy

I look at the sky
I see an airplane as it flies
Is this the way they said Jesus came?
Gone through St. Louis
Gone straightaway
And I hear the winter will cut you quick
If tears were liquor, I'd have drunk myself sick

Woman, are you home?
A house of cards, a frame of bones
Here I am, earthly bound
Said "Hallelujah, I'm going down"
And the River Jordan is deep and wide
I think I see forever across on the other side

I look at the sky
I see a night bird as it flies
Over the old bent cherry trees
Shivering in a row
Down here, the winter will cut you quick
These tears are liquor, and I've drunk myself sick

And the dead of winter will cut you quick
These tears are liquor, and I've drunk myself sick

Riot in My House

There's a riot in my house
Chaos is blossoming
Run and hide, little mouse
Go on and get yourself together
When burnouts by the score
Strung out in metal cages
See Technicolor pour
From every laceration
I realize that I'm slowly coming down with you

Angels fill my room
With what I've scant belief in
When death's metal broom
Comes sweeping through the evening
Get up off the floor
There's hot smoking radiation
From window to the door
In ultra-violent hesitation
I realize that I'm slowly coming down with you

Battle lines appear
Within the broken mirrors
Yet the dogs have no fear
Fighting in the dark grey shadows
Hear the coughing sound
Mama, bring my medication
No harmony is found
While performing levitation
I realize that I'm slowly coming down with you

There's a riot in my house
Chaos is blossoming
Run and hide, little mouse
Go on and get yourself together
From window to the door
There's cold choking strangulation
See Technicolor pour
From every amputation
And realize that I'm slowly coming down with you

Ode to Sad Disco

The sun's tolling bell
Subterranean eyes
A thousand to one
The factory line

Stars outside the window flicker and shine
The hollow headed morning isn't blind
A mountain of nails burn in your hands
Here I give all I am

Gloria
I get down on my knees
Further from my own

A tower of stones
Sympathy's shade
Ride a white horse
The drowned on parade

A diamond headed serpent climbs a vine
See all the lonely children lose their minds
A mountain of dust burns in your mouth
Here there's no north, just south

Gloria
I get down on my knees
Further from my own

Thirst swollen tongue
An Arcadian twist
The sleepwalk is done
Yet the notion persists
Cars outside the window careening by
The hollow headed morning is unkind

Gloria
I get down on my knees
Further from my own

Under a cliff
Darkness denied
Here I have seen the light

Here I have seen the light

Phantasmagoria Blues

I have given to you, Jane
A torn and tattered love
But do you hear the tolling bells
That ring down from above?
Thought I'd rule like Charlemagne
But I've become corrupt
Now I crawl the promenade
To fill my empty cup

And you're free
You're free again
One more time

Now if you found a razor blade
And took it to your wrist
Then I'd be here in my electric chair
Because of this
All last night and night before
I stood on the pier and cried
But I don't want to turn away
For fear of going blind

And you're free
You're free again
One more time

I have given to you, Jane
A bruised and beaten love
But do you see the cold white light
That shines down from above?
Thought I'd rule like Charlemagne
But I've become corrupt
Now I'll crawl the promenade
To fill my empty cup

And you're free
You're free again
One more time

Quiver Syndrome

I turned back toward the factory
With a rail running through my head
And the stain of a rust red romance
Though my Iron Age rose is dead
Will the Lord hold me down 'cause I'm wicked?
Will the Lord hold me down, to my shame?
Will your love it get into me Jesus?
Now I heard you calling out my name

The moon don't smile on Saturday's child
Lying still in Elysian Fields
I don't know what the doctor he did
Now I'm all day long with my body in bed

Plant the seeds of an ivory white lily
Play the ghost of autumn's lullabye
You know the way I came down to the city
Snuffed the love light out of my eyes
I'm knocked back in the alley
With the sweat pouring off my hands
I can tear out a stitch 'cause it's aching
When I'm a shake, shake, shaking I can

The moon don't smile on Saturday's child
Lying still in Elysian Fields
I don't hear what my mother she said
Now I'm all day long with my body in bed

I turn back toward the factory
With a rail running through my head
And the stain of a rust red romance
Though my Iron Age rose is dead
Will the Lord hold me down 'cause I'm wicked?
Will the Lord hold me down, to my shame?
Will your love it get into me, Jesus?
Now I heard you calling out my name

The moon don't smile on Saturday's child
Lying still in Elysian Fields
I don't know what the doctor he did
Now I'm all day long with my body in bed

Harborview Hospital

I walked by Harborview Hospital
I heard the Agnus Dei
Oh, sister of mercy
I've been gone too long to say
And all around this place, I was a sad disgrace

They're singing, they're singing
Away up on the hill
They're building, they're building
A mystical union, beautiful and still
But down here in the dirt, they'll say it doesn't hurt

The devil's ascended
Upon some crystal wings
In the citadel lightning
Splits a cloud of butterflies and fiends
And with a vacant stare, you leave a flower there

They're riding, they're riding
A hellhound down the hill
They're sinking, they're sinking
Into the ocean, beautiful and still
And yet it's hard to leave in wealth or poverty

I walked by Harborview Hospital
And stopped at Ninth and James
Oh, sister of mercy
I've been down too far to say
Are they supposed to be as sick as you and me?

Leviathan

After the deadlock and dazzle
As good as, or better than gold
I lay down my guns on the table
First scarlet, then blue growing cold

Black light and smoke
Making a joke
In the haze of a setting sun

Leviathan waits in the water
Skeletons hide in the trees
The hours crawl by like a spider
Hangman is following me

At sorrow's door
A century more
In the rays of a setting sun

After the deadlock and dazzle
Glitters at night like it's gold
You lay down your heart if you're able
First scarlet, then blue growing cold

Every day a prayer
For what I never knew
But this is one I said for you

Deep Black Vanishing Train

Yellow moon, keep hanging there
And don't you ever come down
Tattered newspaper pages
Are scattered across the ground

Lost on a violent sea
Gone for endless days
I have tried to free myself
But it's been hard to break away

So long light you're bound to fall
Now isn't that a shame
Casting shadows on the wall
Too late to learn another game

Transfixed by what isn't seen
And what will never change
The times I've tried to free myself
It's been hard to look away

It's a deep black vanishing train
Upon a very long track
Standing on a sidewalk in the rain
Hands behind my back

Lost on a violent sea
Day on endless day
I have finally freed myself
But it's been hard to break away

Tiny Grain of Truth

Put the pictures upon the shelf
The ones I tore from magazines and paperbacks
I'm a keep my hurt inside now, love
When it's you I am following

What's done is done is done now
What's done is done is done now
What's done is done is done now
What's done is done

Send down the firewalker
Send down the neon priest
Send down the junky doctor
Send down the shadow king
Down through the heart of the city at night
In black and white

Roll out to a blues funeral
Riding out in a long cortege
Gone with the mariachi
Gone with the butchermen
Gone straight through the eye of a needle at night
In black and white

Straight through the eye of a needle at night

I blurred the pictures and fooled myself
The ones that showed the terminal in negative
I'm a keep my hurt inside now, love
And may you not uncover it

And blood is blood is blood now
And blood is blood is blood now
Yes blood is blood is blood now
And blood is blood
Straight through the eye of a needle at night
In black and white

Send down the firewalker
Send down the neon priest
Send down the junky doctor
Send down the shadow king
Out through the heart of the city at night
In black and white

Black Pudding

(2013)

WHILE I was in Glasgow making a record with Isobel Campbell in 2007, she gave me Duke Garwood's *Emerald Palace* album, and I became a fan of his beautiful, dark, and off-kilter music. When he and I met later that year backstage at London's Bush Hall, it was obvious we were kindred spirits, and the two of us immediately became fast friends. Over the course of the next several years, we sent song ideas back and forth, and in late 2012 we convened at Josh Homme's Pink Duck studio in Burbank, California, with producer Justin Smith to record *Black Pudding*. The finished album contains some of my favorite songs: "Mescalito" is a song I always enjoy playing live, and "Last Rung," "Driver," and "War Memorial" are, to me, as perfect as anything I could ever hope to be a part of.

Pentecostal

Down so long now, Jesus
You know I been down so long
Far turned out and freezing
Won't you carry my body home?

This is why I came
To live a life in a day
With a fire in my head

Who's got the keys to the workhouse?
Satan has locked the door
Got no wings to take us
Up off of that killing floor

Is this why you came?
To handle a snake
And wear a new starry crown?

There's no phoenix rising
To a mansion up on the hill
This albatross I'm riding
Is a train just standing still

This is how I came
With a stench and a stain
To be washed in the blood

War Memorial

Good, have I done good?
I fell on command
Give me my first and last medal

Observed in ritual behind the door
A heavy ivory white door
Where I've come off my hinges

Fire underground, I murdered a sentry there
Without wanting to
Wasn't nothing else to do

Saw a squad of deserters hung from an oak
Saw officers shot from their saddles
Through driving snow and through black smoke

With a pack of feral dogs snapping at my hooves
Eyes rolled back in their heads
The blank blessed eyesight of the dead

Entire battalions snuffed like a spark
Beat like a heart
Drowned by an ocean

Don't tell me the ending of the play
Don't make me look
Look in the mirror

Mescalito

Oh, Mescalito
Many happy returns
You know I'm gonna need you
Gonna need you when I burn
Mescalito

I'll rest in your shadow
You take the sorrow from my heart
And I'll be forever with you
Though the world keeps us apart
Mescalito

Mescalito
What remains is only mud
In the wake of troubled waters
The stain of holy blood
Mescalito

Now the light is dying
We'll soon be dying too
See this hot city summer
Through your eyes so blue

Words on written pages
A pound of coffin nails
Where losing is contagious
I'm tied down to the rails
Mescalito

Many happy returns
You know I'm gonna need you
Gonna need you when I burn
Mescalito
Take the sorrow from my heart
Oh, Mescalito
Though the world keeps us apart
Though the world keeps us apart

Sphinx

It comes to line the road with scarlet flowers
Creatures begin to stir in a rush
Through summer days that last a thousand hours
'Til nighttime drops down in a hush

A choir brightly sing
Shine like an heirloom ring

Within the tomb that has the light interred
In time will she release her prisoner?
No sound at all, the cold is swallowing
The rise and fall of some black hooded thing

A solitary bird
Hides beneath its wing

'Til ivy paints the wall with green again
And all God's creatures start to crawl
From when the harvest moon is vanishing
A lonely crow begins to call

A solitary sun
Sleeps above it all

Last Rung

Why all this gloom in my mind's eye?
Gone to my head like sweet wine
Midnight whispers so quietly
I turn to look, but it might be
A song sung
From the last rung

When night air is thick with misty rain
And your tears spill like champagne
One that's gone that you hoped for
Looks like one that you prayed for
A prayer you hung
From the last rung

Driver

Gonna be your driver
Gonna drive you home

Gonna be your driver
'Cause you're all alone

Death Rides a White Horse

Cut your midnight black hair
And roll you in the dirt
Just slide the needle in
Until it doesn't hurt
If death rides a white horse, then I ain't seen him yet
And I have seen some things that I can't soon forget

When death comes creeping in
Oh, he don't speak a word
The heavens they don't part
No trumpeter is heard
When death comes creeping in

Not feeling any pain
Just the rain upon my skin
As I step down off the train
Let the grinding wheel begin
See the stars without number
They shine without a name
Only God knows where I'm going
Only God can know my shame

Gonna cut your black hair
Gonna roll you in the dirt
Gonna slide the needle in until it doesn't hurt
Cut your midnight black hair

If death rides a white horse, then I ain't seen him yet
If death rides a white horse

Thank You

I left the levee straightaway
But it don't cease its weak complaining
I've been crawling through disease
And all I know is it keeps raining

I see the dead unsteady walking
Hear the radio keep talking
The world on fire
A jubilee
Because the carnival is toxic

Now to go down into the night
With darkness all that I require
I'm a fallen satellite
No hand of god can lift me higher

I thank you baby
Baby please
Thank you for the times we're living
I will fall down to my knees
And I'll be closer then to heaven

You ever seen it rain so hard
That you know the sky is bleeding?
No redemption in the cards
Not only love can break your heart
Believe it

Not only love can break your heart
Believe it

Cold Molly

Cold Molly
Cold cold Molly
Cold Molly ride
Cold Molly
Cold cold Molly
Cold Molly ride

Girl don't you go
Just make my rooster crow
And I'll love you more than heaven
Stay with me, stay
Love me each and every way
And I'll love you more than heaven

Cold Molly
Cold cold Molly
Cold Molly ride
Cold Molly
Cold cold Molly
Cold Molly ride

Heat on up
Heat on up
Just heat on up now, love

Rolling river sound
Gonna hold your body down
Cold Molly straight to heaven
Come out and play
Love me each and every way
And I'll love you more than heaven

Cold Molly
Cold cold Molly
Cold Molly ride
Cold Molly
Cold cold Molly
Cold Molly ride

Heat on up
Heat on up
Won't you heat on up now, love

Shade of the Sun

I stood down in the shade of the sun
To look for some better days
A better day had not yet dawned
Tried to cross where the water was wide
Thought I saw Eden away on the other side

Oh Lord
Lord, don't you hear me?
Oh Lord
Lord, can't you hear me?

I stood down in the shade of the sun
To look for my woman
My woman she was gone
Kept hammering away at the gate
I kept a knocking, but I was far too late

Woman
Woman, don't you hear me
Woman
Woman, don't you hear me

I stood down in the shade of the sun

No Bells on Sunday/Phantom Radio
(2014)

As I've grown older, making records has become much more enjoyable, and instead of creating just the bare bones of what I'm able to, I now make music that is much more in tune with what I myself like listening to.

Even when I make records under my own name, everything I do is a collaboration with others, and these records are no different. They're possible only through my partnership with producer Alain Johannes and Aldo Struyf, who has been the musical director of my band for a decade.

"Dry Iced" is indicative of my long-standing interest in Krautrock and "Floor of the Ocean" is influenced by Factory Records bands Joy Division, Crispy Ambulance, and Section 25. My Leather Nun fetish was mined once again on "Death Trip to Tulsa," and music for the signature tune "I Am the Wolf" was a gift from old friend Duke Garwood.

Dry Iced

I'm sorry
Will these dirty streets absolve their animal?
Through the floor in defeat the sun and stars should fall
Walking, aimlessly walking, walking around
Hear the shadows talking, blue 'cause they're talking, talking me down

Speeding in a long black car from here to Babylon
Heart black like tar, and all my veins are full
Dreaming, ceaselessly dreaming and not asleep
Screaming, I hear somebody screaming and I'm down too deep

Crying on a midnight wire, all dry icicle stoned
I set the fields on fire and still my hands are cold
Echo, in the chamber an echo, echoing on
In danger the alien stranger to eternity's gone

I'm sorry
Will these city streets absolve their animal?
To the dirt in defeat the sun and stars should fall
Walking, aimlessly walking, walking around
Talking, blue shadows talking, talking me down
I'm sorry
I'm sorry
I'm sorry

No Bells on Sunday

Now the vanishing's begun
When drowning late at night
The blown glass setting sun weeps electric light
A mirror holds no gaze, just a beacon dying
All I know, in a way, I think it's me that crying

No bells on Sunday, no wings to fly
To the ground god bless you
I'm missing you tonight
It's always the same, standing out in the rain
It comes down to break me
I'm praying just the same
It comes down to break me
I'm praying just the same

Sad Lover

I watch as my sad lover dreams
On a wave of swirling hurricane disaster
With a bullet for the ghost following after
I watch as my sad lover dreams

I hate when the red sun goes down
And burns a lonely shadow into pavement
And the breaking of my heart I can't evade it
I hate when that red sun goes down

I pray for my sad lover's dream
On a wave of swirling Novocain and laughter
And tears the only gift following after
I pray for my sad lover's dream
I pray for my sad lover's dream

Jonas Pap

Where is the sound I was hearing in my head?
Where is the wine? Gone to my head

Hey now, everybody listen, everybody listen to the song of Pap
Hey now, everybody listen, everybody listen to the song of Pap

Jonas Pap, Jonas Pap
Sloppy with his drink in his Christmas cap
He ain't no sucker, he ain't no sap
Everybody sing the song of Pap

Jonas Pap is a man
He's a brave man
Jonas Pap is a man
He's a brave man

Where is the song I was hearing in my head?
Where is the wine? Gone to my head

Jonas Pap is a man
He's a brave man
Jonas Pap is a man
He's a brave man
Jonas Pap is a man
He's a brave man

Hey now, everybody listen, everybody listen to the song of Pap

Smokestackmagic

Smokestack magic has dusted my lungs
Freakishly tragic, gracelessly numb
TV boy, TV girl
Stay on your TV set until the end of the world
I came awake and heard the voice of Jesus Christ
You make me feel like I've already died
Smokestack magic painfully pure
I was in transit now I'm unsure
Now I'm unsure now I'm unsure
Smokestack magic shadowy dog
Dig through to China bury it all
I came awake and heard the voice of Jesus Christ
You make me feel like I've already died
Smokestack magic too far from home
Nothing but static phantom radio
And nail into bone nail into bone
Smokestack magic dusted my lungs
Freakishly tragic gracelessly numb
I came awake and heard the voice of Jesus Christ
You make me feel like I've already died
Smokestack magic nail into bone

Harvest Home

Happy in my harvest home
Walking the floor with the ghosts all alone
Happy that I'm made of stone
The grief that I cause is my cause to atone
Now black is a color, black is my name
When I need something to help me chase the devil away

The house on fire
The fraying high wire
Nothing to say
The sky so grey
I reap, I sow
My harvest
My home

Judgement Time

She said it's the time of judgement
I'm a rolling holy down a dirty river
In a dream I heard Gabriel's trumpet
Lord and I was blistered
Just a strung out angel
I saw the feet of pilgrims bleeding
Saw whole cities drowning
Saw whole armies dying
A reverie of starlings on my shoulder
On the shoulder of a highway
Judgement time is near
Judgement time is near
Watch those stars above, they're falling
And when the sky is falling
It falls like heaven's rain
She said it's the time of judgement
I'm a rolling holy down a dirty river
Oh oh, judgement time is near
Oh oh, judgement time is near
Oh oh, judgement time is near
Oh oh, judgement time is near

Floor of the Ocean

Hard times
Walking in the sunshine
Crawling through a landslide
Guilty of some old crimes
Clear eyes
Can't avoid the searchlight
Hope that they don't find me
Find me where I'm lying

Scars, bone and blood
Iron, clay and mud
Can I find my way?
Can I mine my way
Through the core of emotion?

Dumpsite
Out along the roadside
Look into the cold sky
Look into your mind's eye
Midnight
Can't escape the searchlight
Hope that they don't catch me
Catch me where I'm riding

Scars, bone and blood
Iron, clay and mud
Gonna find my way
Gonna mine my way
Through the floor of the ocean

Hard times
Walking in the sunshine
Crawling through a landslide
Guilty of some old crimes
Clear eyes
Can't avoid the searchlight
Hope that they don't find me
Find me where I'm lying

Scars, bone and blood
Iron, clay and mud
Can I find my way?
Can I mine my way
Through the core of emotion?
Scars, bone and blood
Iron, clay and mud
Gonna find my way
Gonna mine my way
Through the floor of the ocean

The Killing Season

The killing season it's beginning
I feel your hands around my throat
You either lose or come up winning
I wear my old grey overcoat

Now paint it Mary, paint it black
Tonight they hang Jerry
Tonight they hang Jack
When this killing season's over
I'll never say your name again
And if I smell the perfume of
The perfume of your blood
I know it's just the incense
Incense of my drug

Do you hear the children speaking backward?
Their bodies float above the bed
Who sings a song that isn't sung?
My soul's in traction
Cops and criminals and all that crawl
Get into action
Smelling the incense of, the perfume of your blood
Smelling the incense of, the perfume of my drug

The brick and mortar start to pound
A powder in the air like anthrax
Brought six white horses down
When this cold dark night is over
There ain't nobody left around

Now paint it Mary, paint it black
Tonight they hang Jerry
Tonight they hang Jack
And when this fever dream has ended
I'll never come this way again
And if I smell the perfume of
The perfume of your blood
I know it's just the incense
Incense of my drug

The killing season it's beginning
Skeletal hands are on my throat
Someone will lose somebody's winnings
I wear my old grey overcoat
I wear my old grey overcoat

Seventh Day

How the smoke get in my eye
Awake to find the orchid died
Coincidence the seventh day
I guess that I'll be on my way

Rolling down the streets of gold
Tombstones and bullet holes
Now you're gonna ride alone in danger
Hang the phone up on the wall
Though I hate to leave you, doll
On the face of one and all a stranger

Let the lonely dance begin
As the night is vanishing
If you dare to let me in, it's danger
Don't you sleep in poppy fields
Don't you let the mask conceal
Don't you ever do a deal with strangers

How the blood get in my eye
Awake to find the sun has died
Find the key, unlock my cage
Break the back that bore my rage
In the dirt and choking sin
Let the freezing night begin
Try to rise above the din, it stains ya
Like the soldier on the wall
Like the lonely lemur call
Like the thing that creep and crawl, it's danger

I Am the Wolf

I am the wolf
Without a pack
Banished so long ago
I've survived on another's kill
And on my shadow home

All I've learned is that poison will sting
No one remembers the names of martyrs or kings
No one remembers much of anything
That came this way before

I am the wolf
Combing the beach
Too hungry to shy away
The carcass of a leviathan
Sways gently on the waves

I hope this shelter is enough to keep me warm
Upstairs the heaven's giving birth to winter's storm
But I've been dying since the day I was born
That much I know is true

I am the wolf
High, wild and free
A picture on a shelf
I burn this house down to the ashes
A law unto myself

All I've learned is that poison will sting
No one remembers the names of martyrs or kings
No one remembers much of anything
That came this way before
That came this way before

I am the wolf
I am the wolf
I am the wolf

Torn Red Heart

You don't love me
What's to love anyway?
You don't love me
Would love be my saving grace?
You don't love me

It's delirium
It's a childlike dream then it fades away
It's illusion
Would love put me in my place?
The illusion
The delirium
The delusion
I'm going nowhere
Now I'm going nowhere

You don't love me
What's to love anyway?
You don't love me
Would love be my saving grace?
You don't love me
Now I'm going nowhere
I'm going nowhere
I'm going nowhere
With my torn red heart
With my torn red heart
With my torn red heart
With my torn red heart

Waltzing in Blue

Oh, what can I say?
I'm bleeding for you
Only a scratch
Waltzing in blue
Oh, I can't see the day
Blinded by you
Faded away
Waltzing in blue
No, nobody home
They've gone out to play
Gone to the ball
Psychoses and all
And love
Love's fevered stain
Hour by hour
Is down to decay
Oh, what can I say?
Still haunted by you
Quiet as a ghost
Waltzing in blue
Waltzing in blue
Waltzing in blue

The Wild People

My sin, my sin
Is done and it won't be forgiven
I'm gone, I'm gone
I'm going where the wild people living
Gone where the wild
Wild people living
So long alone
Close to the bone
They kill the messenger
They kill the taxman waiting in line
They kill the passenger
Where the train and taxi collide

A holiday has come
My mind has escaped into hiding
I've shot away my life
Out where the wild people riding
Out where the wild
Wild people riding
So long alone
Close to the bone
Mama mama ma please
Please don't kill the messenger man
Mama mama ma please
Please don't kill the passenger man

Saturday I'm sick
I'm sick with a virus descending
Burn Sunday to the quick
To the quick with a match on a mile long stick
My sin, my sin
Is done and it won't be forgiven
I'm gone, I'm gone
I'm going where the wild people living
Gone where the wild
Wild people living
So long alone
Close to the bone
Mama mama ma please
Please don't kill the messenger man
Mama mama ma please
Please don't kill the passenger man

Death Trip to Tulsa

High high high
Away up in the sun
Waiting for you doctor
Are you gonna come?
My my my
Rolling in the sound
Thinking 'bout you baby
Are you gonna drown?

Went up to the station
Found a horror scene
Fell into the strangest
Lonely, lonely dream

The lord made me a poor man
The lord made me a thief
A thousand miles of midnight
To shine beyond belief
It's my last trip to the corner
Now how am I gonna breathe?
A child upon this wasteland
The teeth of the disease

Went out on location
Found a horror scene
Fell into the strangest
Lonely, lonely dream

High high high
Away up in the air
I look for you baby
But you ain't never there
Death trip to Tulsa

You know I might suffer some
Waiting for you doctor
Are you gonna come?

Went down to the nation
Found a horror scene
Fell into the strangest
Lonely lonely
Lonely lonely dream

High high high
Away up in the sun
Away up in the sun
Away up in the sun

Gargoyle
(2017)

ANOTHER YEAR, another record . . . looking back over them, it seems as though I've been driving the same road over and over, with only slight variations on the map. The same themes of loss, longing, mortality, and chemical dependence are all here again.

I enjoyed writing the words for "Blue Blue Sea," "Beehive," and "Emperor" because they seem to have a slightly more lighthearted feel than my songs usually do, and "Old Swan" is almost completely devoid of darkness, which might be a first for me.

Death's Head Tattoo

Wild thing
See the monkey in the jungle swing
Canary in the cavern sing
That the devil lives in anything

C'mon, people
You know that I ain't got the wherewithal
When California starts to crawl
Makes a poor man leave his home

And if I cry for you baby
Your death's head tattoo made me
Pray for the last one standing
Holding a loaded gun
I can see her there under the golden sun

Wild thing
See the man up on the gallows swing
See the creature walking through the weeds
In a garden grown from evil seeds

C'mon, people
You know I can't afford to reconcile
When California starts to crawl
Makes a poor child leave its home

And if I cry for you baby
Your death's head tattoo made me
Pray for the last one standing
Holding a loaded gun
I can see her there under the golden sun

Better the devil you know
Than the one that you don't
Better the devil you know
Than the one that you don't

C'mon, people
You know that I ain't got the wherewithal
When California starts to crawl
Makes a poor man leave his home

And if I cry for you baby
Your death's head tattoo made me
Pray for the last one standing
Holding a loaded gun
I can see her there under the golden sun

Nocturne

Red lights
X-ray vision
That lonely drug is in my veins
Blood stained
Indecision
And holiness is burned away
Midnight
Midnight calling
To color me insane

Still life with roses in a vase
Thorn is in your hand
Unsent letters in a box
Frozen where you stand

Do you miss me, miss me darling?
God knows I'm missing you
Somewhere there's two trains colliding
That's what this sickness brought me to

Dead right
All night
When you feel the serpent strike
Nocturne

Black light
House of mirrors
The heavens open up and bleed
Face down
Drifting backward
A lonely river to the sea
Midnight
Midnight calling
Coloring my dreams

Anchor chained around your neck
Crisis in your hand
Whispering behind your back
Falling where you stand

Do you miss me, miss me darling?
God knows I'm missing you
I can see two cars colliding
That's what this sickness brought me to

Do you miss me, miss me darling?
Do you know I'm missing you?
Can't you see the world is ended?
That's what this damage took me to

Dead right
All night
When you feel the spider bite
Nocturne

Do you miss me, miss me darling?
God knows I'm missing you
I can see two worlds colliding
That's what this sickness brought me to

Dead right
All night
When you feel the serpent strike
Nocturne

Blue Blue Sea

Lord of fire in the sky
Getting level, neon devil
Holy holy in my mind
To abide and crucify
With blue blue sea
Far away

Gargoyle perched on gothic spire
Amplifier, getting higher
Who put Lucifer in harness?
All dishonored past discarded
And blue blue sea
Far away

Beehive

Scenes of dying light
Everywhere through a firecracker summer
Suddenly alone in a beehive
With a spider crawling along my spine

Blue water down from the mountains
Washed across the killing floor
Blood rushing up from a fountain
Can't undo a thing no more
I drag my chair to the window
And listen to the swarm

Beehive
Beehive
Honey just gets me stoned when I'm living
Bell rung
And stung
Honey just gets me stoned
Just gets me stoned

Scenes of dying love
In my head buzzed as a bees' nest
Hanging down from above
Everywhere I look it's a bummer

Gasoline in cool, cool water
I'm lying on a cooling board
Lightning coming out of the speakers
Wanna hear that sound some more
Press my body against the window
In an electric storm

Beehive
Beehive
Honey just gets me stoned when I'm living
Bell rung
And stung
Honey just gets me stoned
Just gets me stoned
Honey just gets me stoned

Sister

Those spirits in the wood
I can't count them all
Run me down the briar
Chase me 'til I fall
The dead white witch's gaze
Mirrors mine at night
Dares my soul to sleep
Wants my soul to keep

Sister
Sister of mine
Set the sky on fire
The savage kingdom is blind

Those spirits in the wood
I can't name them all
Place me in a hood
Walk me to the wall
All these lonely things
I have held so near
You glean just the same
Yet they're never here

Sister
Sister of mine
Set the sky on fire
The savage kingdom is blind

The morphine drugged the man who marooned
The captain steered the ship to ruin
The crow released the crimson balloon
The morphine drugged the man who marooned

Emperor

I awoke in fright
No love, no one to save me
Night after night
So lonely, lonely baby
Why can't I get right?
All these demons to enslave me
Who is left to fight?
Just the emperor
Just the emperor
Just the emperor

On the water still
My boat violently shaking
I need another pill
Another bitter pill to wake me
Upon the window sill
The cat silently quaking
Who is left to kill?
Just the emperor
Just the emperor
Just the emperor

The battlefield is crossed
The flag and castle falling
Is the army lost?
Command no longer calling
Into an early frost
A few survivors crawling
Who could know the cost?
Just the emperor
Just the emperor
Just the emperor

Goodbye to Beauty

On the marble street
A procession spills in
At the white sea wall
Waves crash and crash again
Darkness shining
Then disappearing
Day follows night, night follows day
Comes like a stranger, then it drifts away
Day follows night, night follows day

Goodbye
Goodbye to beauty
Goodbye to beauty

In a mansion above
The ceremony begins
On a bandstand below
The conductor laments
The dogs are whining
Something's changing
Day follows night, night follows day
Makes like a friend before it slips away
Day follows night, night follows day

Goodbye
Goodbye to beauty
Goodbye to beauty

Drunk on Destruction

Drunk on destruction
Feel I'm fading away
Drunk, drunk on destruction
Feel I'm fading away

Death is my due
How I never wondered
Turning the screw
Into the dirt
And now I'm going under
A silver haze bleeds from the sun
I am the target and the gun

This flawed construction
Feel I'm fading away
Drunk on destruction
Feel I'm fading away
La la la la la la

Black out the day
And every constellation
The driving rain has come to drown
All illumination
A sip of bitterness at first
Becomes unending with its thirst

Drunk on destruction
Feel, I feel I'm fading away
Drunk, drunk on destruction
Feel I'm fading away

Death is my due
How I never wondered

First Day of Winter

There's nothing left in this town
Just the ghosts that drag me around
In sorrow

Been searching with these tombstone eyes
Looking for a new disguise
In sorrow

Blinded by these icy tears
And a photograph of you my dear
In sorrow

See the rain down window run
Chills my veins now it's begun
The first day of winter

Old Swan

Clean
New roads unfurled
Light of the world
Redeemed
Your humble child
Don't leave me here
Let me come with you

And though my soul is not worth saving
My mistress and my queen
Your spirit is larger than my sin

It does not lie
It does not lie

In this faith that we live and die
I give myself to you

Sustained
No need to explain
Fade into the sun
The evening kisses your rays

Sweet mother
Queen of the world
I'm free
Free at last

Dear Mother
Queen of earth and air
Let cool water flow
Sweet mother
Queen of the world
Let cool water flow

Claim this land
North south east west
To the wind you dance
Sweet mother
I give myself to you
And have no other
Have no other than you

Clean
Through the eternal
Through dead seasons
Sail to the sun
My mother and my queen
Honest and serene

Praise God
God in everything
God in everyone
Way up
Way up high
Way up high mama
All my darkness cleaned away
Sweet mother
Sweet sweet mother
Sweet mother
Queen of the world
Take me in your arms
Let me live again
Clean

One-offs and Collaborations

THESE ARE various B-sides, one-offs, and lyrics I wrote for other people's records: Unkle, Moby, Earth, Isobel Campbell, Creature with the Atom Brain, Dave Clarke, Ten Commandos, Humanist, Mad Season, and others.

Black Rider Run

Black rider run
Black rider run
Look what you done
Now you can find your way through the underworld
Or dissolve in the sun

Black rider run

You belong to a spider brother
Can't wash the stain away
To the moon set a moth to flutter
In a golden mountain to stay

Black rider run
Look what you've done
Now you can find your way through the underworld
Or burn in the sun
Black rider run

You've been bit by a spider brother
Can't wash the blood away
To the moon set a moth to flutter
In a hollow mountain to stay

You belong to a spider brother
Can't wash the stain away
To the moon set a moth to flutter
In a golden mountain to stay

Song #1

You can go anywhere you want
The cat's claw holds a monkey paw
Rusty shade of a razor blade
Rainstorm on the floorboard

Danger is as danger does
Look out love, I'm dangerous
Six miles down to the underground
World war in the fourth form

Danger is as danger does
Look out love, I'm dangerous
Six miles down to the underground
World war in the fourth form

You're stolen fire
On the high wire

That's the rite of the hunter
The night of the hunter

Crawl Like a Dog

When I'm lost slipping away
Jesus can't you save me from another hard day
Crawl like a dog nothing to say
I can't remember to remember my name

When I'm lost slipping away
Crawl like a dog nothing to say
I can't remember to remember my name

When I'm lost slipping away
Jesus can't you save me from another hard day
Crawl like a dog nothing to say
I can't remember to remember my name

Mirrored

You see yourself
In your true love's eyes
As something strange
Something blind

Close the window
And lay down to sleep
With graveyard scenes
In violent dreams

And love doesn't see a thing
Love makes a marionette
Dance on silver strings
There's a mirror in your true love's eyes

Remember where those sparks were thrown
Then think of me as well
As the light starts fading
And his fingers crawl through your dark hair

Here's where you learn something
What makes the marionette
Dance on silver strings
Dance in the mirror of your true love's eyes

One reflection sees the other blind
Look deep in each
Two tombstones shine
Close the window and lay down to sleep
With graveyard scenes
In violent dreams

And everywhere that sparks are thrown
Then think of me as well
As the light starts fading
And his fingers crawl through your dark hair

My love is no living thing
My love makes a marionette
Dance on silver strings

And there's a mirror
In my true love's eyes

Another Night Out

Lift the wheels up from the roadway
Close your sparrow's glassy eyes
And walk upon the water
Once more for me
Are those dead diamonds baby?
Or are they stars gone to sleep?
So low that you might miss me
Slowly fades the light
So low that you might miss me
Slowly fades the light
Wait for the spring
And to this thing I do surrender
To the darkest sin
I climb with the vine
On a graveyard train pulling away
Drowning to dive
Down full fathom five
To wear the hollow crown
To haunt the hollow trees

And what from heaven's tongue is heard
Through the veins
Love sustained
Another night out
So low that you might miss me
Slowly fades the light
Another night out
Another night out
Wait for the spring
And to this thing I give myself
On a graveyard train pulling away
Down into heaven
Down into heaven

Down into heaven
Blue, blue heaven
To wear the hollow crown
To haunt the hollow trees
To wear the hollow crown
To haunt the hollow trees

Revolver

Now after all
Don't it feel like nothing?
Like walking away
Like a mouthful of rain
At twelve o'clock a bell starts ringing
A dog starts barking
And you're still missing
Still missing something
You've never known what it was

And I'm not one for thinking twice
But I know this much is true
The earth will turn
And the powder burn
And you are my revolver

Just waking up, some dogs start barking
A bell starts ringing
And you're still missing
And after all, don't it feel like nothing?
Like walking away
Like a mouthful of rain
I'm holding on 'cause you're my revolver
And I dreamed of it ending
In a violent way

Black River

A cold black river running
Who knows which way it's gone?
I feel the half that is missing
Until the river flows back to me

Come outside into the sun
I know in time your will be done
And mine like a black river running

It's dark
Dark in my motel room
Daylight comes under the door
And shines
Shines on my dirty shoes
A prayer, silence, and nothing more

Come outside into the sun
I know in time your will be done
And mine just keeps on running

A cold black river running
Who knows which way it's gone?
I feel the half that is missing
Until river flows back to me
Until river flows back to me

There Is a Serpent Coming

I see behemoth coming
I see a serpent coming
I see a beast is coming
I see a deadly heat is coming

All praise and exaltation
Black train I ride has left the station
New revelation time
So deep, so deep and deadly

New revelation time
So deep, so deep, so deep and deadly
Children, children get ready
Better get ready
New revelation time
Shadow revelator
Old black diamond in my eye

I see all that creep and crawl is coming
All praise and exaltation
Black train I ride has left the station
New revelation time
So primitive and deadly
New revelation time
So deep, so deep, so deep and deadly
Children, children get ready
You better get ready
New revelation time
Shadow revelator
Old black diamond in my eye

That train I ride has left the station

The Lonely Night

Here come the lonely night
Can't escape my mind

From a broken bough, fall into finite space
With the roof torn down, this house is an empty place
So tired of wandering around and starting over
No garden grows here now, just the one-leaf clover
And when the window's shuttered, it's always dark inside
Sometimes the pain is absurd, still it's what fate decides
Thought I saw Jesus come down dressed like a soldier
I used to cry like a clown and now I'm older
Here come the lonely night
I can't escape my mind

The grinding wheel turns and the heavens burn
As the pilot ignites is a lesson learned
A sullen look of concern, it might make you sad
Like the fluttering bird in a dream you had
Here come the lonely night
I can't escape my mind
I saw Jesus come down dressed like a soldier
Once I cried like, like a clown, now I'm older
Here come the lonely night
Can't escape my mind

Kingdom

I'm riding through the kingdom
A ghost is riding by my side
As we roll up to the kingdom
Ours is just to ride or die

There is no medicine to cure us
There is no medicine to take
Beware the shark below the surface
Beware the love that you forsake

Keep a-riding
Keep a-riding baby
Keep a-riding
Keep a-riding baby

Death tripping through the kingdom
Death is riding by my side
We are rolling through the kingdom
Ours is just to ride or die

Doctor are you gonna cure us?
Give us some medicine to take
I am the shark below the surface
I am the love that you forsake

Mama, turn your floodlights on
Let them radiate
Turn your floodlights on
Let them radiate

Gospel

Well my mother, my father too
They have, have gone home to be with god
To lay their troubles down

You know my sister and brother too
They have gone home to be with god
They have gone home to lay their burdens down

All my friends, relations too
Have all gone home to be with god
They've gone home to lay their suffering down

Mister conductor let me ride the train
Mister conductor let me get on board the train

Skull

The astral body's last deal
It's a nightmare made real
Ghost plane on the runway
Ghost ship gone down

Hook a hardwire to my skull
There's a dream dancing on and on
Find a flower growing from my skull
Wrap it in linen, give it to my baby
The astral body's last deal
It's the lightning made real

Is it over?
Think it over
I think you better think it over baby
Is it over?
Think it over
I think you better think it over baby

The astral body's last deal
It's a nightmare made real

See the horns growing from my skull
There's a fire burning on and on
Find a flower growing from my skull
Wrap it in linen, give it to my baby

Is it over?
Think it over
I think you better think it over baby
Is it over?
Think it over
I think you better think it over baby

Hook a hardwire to my skull
There's a dream dancing on and on
Find a flower growing from my skull
Wrap it in linen, give it to my baby

Staring Down the Dust

Staring down the dust
Shooting the arrow of death
The mourning of paradise lost
Sing with me under your breath

Take me through the garden
Take me through the dark
Baby beg your pardon
Keep me from coming apart

The swinging of a chain
Facing the firing line
Who will remember your name?
Drowning the ashes in wine

Staring down the dust
Walking all alone
Take it as far as you must
Taking it clear to the bone

I can't quiet my mind
I wouldn't tell no lie

Staring down the dust
Kissing the angel of death
Praying your will isn't crushed
Singing it under your breath
Staring down the dust
Mourning of paradise lost
Shooting the arrow of death
Sing with me under your breath

I can't quiet my mind
I wouldn't tell no lie

Staring down the dust

Locomotive

No sleep
Your countenance fallen
White as a sheet
In the face of the rain grown colder
Wallflower waltzing
Locomotive crawling
Blood on the wheels where the rust don't stain
Your self chosen cure is your self chosen pain

No time to ride
On the back of a beast such as suicide
Johnny come lately
The black light suits you baby

Too sweet
It's there for the killing
Lying there at your feet
But the face in the mirror's grown older
A bell's distant ringing
A scorpion stinging
The wheel's making noise but your mind don't care
The world's screaming in like you're not even there

You slide inside
To the back of a train they call suicide
Johnny come lately
You know the black light suits you, baby

Black Book of Fear

Disconnected
Far above the ground
You're too close to hear
That thundering sound

Neglected
Behind castle wall
It's your high wire walk
It's your kingdom to fall

Raining
God give up the rain
The way it comes down
Is a goddamn shame
Fading
Fading to blue
As distant as time
As cold as the moon

This is the room where a crime scene was staged
Opened a black book of fear and tore out a page
This is a house where a crime scene was staged

One of these days we'll be walking in the sun
Some simple day that has not yet begun
In one of these visions the devil got away
In one of these dreams the dirt didn't stain

This is a house where a crime scene was staged
Opened a black book of fear and tore out a page
This is a room where a crime scene was staged

Raining
God give up the rain
The way it comes down is a goddamn shame
Fading
Fading to blue
As distant as time
As cold as the moon

This is a room where a crime scene was staged
Opened a black book of fear and tore out a page
This is a house where a crime scene was staged

Neglected
Behind castle wall
It's your high wire walk
It's your kingdom to fall
Raining
God give up the rain
The way it comes down is a goddamn shame

Slip Away

Born of the water
Born of the flame
This life is a monster
Don't you know it's name?
The house it is wooden
The house it is stone
The proud broken hearted
And close to the bone
Once you had a nightmare
And then it came to pass
Grey is the sky in the morning
Green is the grass covering the grave

Just a slip away
Just a slip away

Down to the water
Drawn to the flame
This life'll leave you crippled
Don't you know the game?
Once you woke up choking
But then you held it down
Dry as the sand in the desert
Black as the clouds covering the sun

Untitled Lullaby

Until you sleep
And your fingers are finally still
I'm going to stay awake all night

Children don't weep
All will be quiet in time
An overcoat of prayers and lullabies

La la la la la la la la la la
So far to climb
So hard to learn
La la la la la la la la la la

It's a dime for a tin whistle and a cigarette
Goddamned if you listen but what else do you get?

La la la la la la la la la la
So far to climb
So hard to learn

Until you sleep
And your fingers are finally still
I'm bound to stay awake all night

Burning Jacob's Ladder

Dreams stripped down beyond firelight
I would go over, but my only coat's off-white
And seeing things unreal
God knows what that stained
And what comes crawling back again
Tears are harbored
Down to the thorny altar
I'm afraid I might fade away

Here's to the blood we sing and burn
A thousand blackbirds on a string return
There's a solitary sun too high
Gone without the chosen one, goodbye
Ashes scatter
Burning Jacob's ladder
I'm afraid I might fade away

Here's to the blood we sing and burn
A thousand blackbirds on a string return
There's a solitary sun too high
Gone without the chosen one, goodbye
Rage untethered
The soul a stony desert
I'm afraid I might fade away

Dreams stripped down beyond firelight
I would go over, but my only coat's off-white
And seeing things unreal
God knows what that stained
And what comes crawling back again
Ashes scatter
Burning Jacob's ladder
I'm afraid I might fade away

Mud Pink Skag

Better keep moving and both eyes open
Keep it down and off you go
Is it heavy yet baby?
Hear me fade in stereo

Because a killer at the window
Tries to catch you while you rest
It's a suffering in DayGlo
Wakes a demon in your chest

A Cinderella in the midnight
Her beauty covered in a landslide
Is still walking on the nightline
Oh so heavy

Want to go on, but you're too nervous
Get to swing that weight around
Cause when you're swaying, little baby
You like to tear those heavens down

They all join in where she started
She leaves 'em crying when she goes
And they move like the retarded
All getting heavy

You're sleeping when you smile
And you smile when you're sick
Keep on dreaming when you kick
When to kick is heavy
Heavy

I see you sway with eyes half open
Better keep moving, there you go
There's a blackout at mid-morning
You hear me fade in stereo

And you're sleeping when you smile
And trying when you're sick
Cause a light up in the window
Wakes a demon when you kick
A Cinderella in the midnight
Her beauty covered by a landslide
Is still walking on the nightline
Oh, getting heavy
Heavy

The Monochrome Sun

The sun bleeds in monochrome
Sirens in the air
Through misery and ritual
A newborn star appears

An orphan crying for its mother
Who will never come
To free one horse and blind another
A demon loads a gun

Too many splinters in my mind
Too many splendors for my eyes

Who will make the sky alight
The hunchback of desire?
The soldier in the underground?
Who'll set the earth on fire?

A child waits for its mother
And it waits in vain
For god to bring the dead to life
Blessed be his name

Come down from your forest
Golden headed lion
What lives inside of me is death
What lives in you divine

Eternity spent for a mother
Who had never come
So crystallized I have no other
A demon with a gun

Too many splinters in my mind

Love Story

What's on the windowpane
Was once heaven's rain
Is only a shame
Now I'm sinking

Don't love something too much
Because then the vein is open
It'll pour out a river
When you're already drowning

Close the book if the story's over
Cash out at curtain call
This is clearly the fall
I won't get up from

Credits

ALBUMS

Above (Mad Season)

All songs published by Drive Music Publishing o/b/o Ripplestick Music, Jumpin' Cat Music, Inside Passage Music o/b/o Wrecking Ball Music, M. Marie Music

Words and music by Mark Lanegan, Michael McCready, Barrett Martin, and John Baker Saunders

Except:

"Black Book of Fear"

Published by Drive Music Publishing o/b/o Ripplestick Music, Jumpin' Cat Music, Inside Passage Music o/b/o Wrecking Ball Music, M. Marie Music, Night Garden Music administered by Music-Warner Tamerlane

Words and music by Mark Lanegan, Michael McCready, Barrett Martin, John Baker Saunders, and Peter Buck

All Rights Reserved. Used by Permission.

Black Pudding

All songs published by Drive Music Publishing o/b/o Ripplestick Music, Embassy Music Corporation/Music Sales

Words and music by Mark Lanegan and Duke Garwood

Except:

"Shade of the Sun"

Published by Drive Music Publishing o/b/o Ripplestick Music

Words and music by Mark Lanegan

All Rights Reserved. Used by Permission.

Blues Funeral

All songs published by Drive Music Publishing o/b/o Ripplestick Music

Words and music by Mark Lanegan

All Rights Reserved. Used by Permission.

Broken (Soulsavers)

All songs published by Drive Music
  Publishing o/b/o Ripplestick
  Music, BMG Platinum Songs US
Words and music by Mark Lanegan,
  Ian Glover, and Rich Machin
Except:
"Death Bells"
"Shadows Fall"
Published by Drive Music Publishing
  o/b/o Ripplestick Music, BMG
  Platinum Songs US, Richard
  Warren Publishing Designee
Words and music by Mark Lanegan,
  Ian Glover, Rich Machin, and
  Richard Warren
All Rights Reserved. Used by
  Permission.

Bubblegum

All songs published by EMI
  Blackwood Music, Inc.
Words and music by Mark Lanegan
Except:
"Hit the City"
Published by EMI Blackwood Music,
  Inc. and Songs of Windswept
  o/b/o Justice Artists Music
Words and music by Mark Lanegan
  and Randall Jamail
All Rights Reserved. Used by
  Permission.

Field Songs

All songs published by Songs of
  Windswept o/b/o Justice Artists
  Music

Words and music by Mark Lanegan
Except:
"Kimiko's Dream House"
Published by Songs of Windswept
  o/b/o Justice Artists Music
Words and music by Mark Lanegan
  and Jeffrey Pierce
"Pill Hill Serenade"
Published by Songs of Windswept
  o/b/o Justice Artists Music
Words and music by Mark Lanegan
  and Michael Johnson
All Rights Reserved. Used by
  Permission

Gargoyle

All songs published by Drive Music
  Publishing o/b/o Ripplestick
  Music, Channel This Music
Words and music by Mark Lanegan
  and Alain Johannes
Except:
"Beehive"
"Drunk on Destruction"
"Goodbye to Beauty"
"Nocturne"
"Old Swan"
Published by Drive Music Publish-
  ing o/b/o Ripplestick Music, Rob
  Marshall Publishing Designee
Words and music by Mark Lanegan
  and Rob Marshall
"Deaths Head Tattoo"
Published by Drive Music Publishing
  o/b/o Ripplestick Music, Channel
  This Music, Rob Marshall Publish-
  ing Designee

Words and music by Mark Lanegan,
Alain Johannes, and Rob Marshall
All Rights Reserved. Used by
Permission.

Has God Seen My Shadow?

All songs published by Drive Music
Publishing o/b/o Ripplestick Music
Words and music by Mark Lanegan
Except:
"Blues for D"
Published by Drive Music
Publishing o/b/o Ripplestick
Music, Stupidditties Music c/o
BMG Gold Songs
Words and music by Mark Lanegan
and Ben Shepherd
All Rights Reserved. Used by
Permission.

Here Comes That Weird Chill

All songs published by EMI Black-
wood Music, Inc.
Words and music by Mark Lanegan
Except:
"Skeletal History"
Published by EMI Blackwood Music,
Inc.
Words and music by Mark Lanegan,
Josh Homme, and Nick Olivieri
"Lexington Slow Down"
Published by EMI Blackwood Music,
Inc., Richitti Music
Words and music by Mark Lanegan
and Keni Richards
"On the Steps of the Cathedral"

Published by EMI Blackwood Music,
Inc., Chris Goss Publishing
Designee
Words and music by Mark Lanegan
and Chris Goss
All Rights Reserved. Used by
Permission.

Houston Publishing Demos

All songs published by Drive Music
Publishing o/b/o Ripplestick
Music, Songs of Windswept o/b/o
Justice Artists Music
Words and music: Mark Lanegan and
Randall Jamail
All Rights Reserved. Used by
Permission.

It's Not How Far You Fall, It's the Way You Land (Soulsavers)

All songs published by EMI
Blackwood Music, Inc., BMG
Platinum Songs US
Words and music by Mark Lanegan,
Ian Glover, and Rich Machin
All Rights Reserved. Used by
Permission.

No Bells on Sunday

All songs published by Drive Music
Publishing o/b/o Ripplestick
Music
Words and music by Mark Lanegan
All Rights Reserved. Used by
Permission.

Phantom Radio
All songs published by Drive Music
  Publishing o/b/o Ripplestick
  Music
Words and music by Mark Lanegan
Except:
"Harvest Home"
Published by Drive Music Publishing
  o/b/o Ripplestick Music, Channel
  This Music
Words and music by Mark Lanegan
  and Alain Johannes
"The Killing Season"
Published by Drive Music Publishing
  o/b/o Ripplestick Music, Down-
  town Publishing
Words and music by Mark Lanegan
  and Sietse Van Gorkom
All Rights Reserved. Used by
  Permission.

Scraps at Midnight
All songs published by EMI Black-
  wood Music, Inc.
Words and music by Mark Lanegan
Except:
"Because of This"
"Bell Black Ocean"
"Praying Ground"
Published by EMI Blackwood Music,
  Inc., No One Cares Music, Richitti
  Music
Words and music by Mark Lanegan,
  Michael Johnson, and Keni
  Richards
"Last One in the World"

"Stay"
"Waiting on a Train"
Published by EMI Blackwood Music,
  Inc., No One Cares Music
Words and music by Mark Lanegan
  and Michael Johnson
All Rights Reserved. Used by
  Permission.

The Winding Sheet
All songs published by EMI
  Blackwood Music, Inc., No One
  Cares Music
Words and music by Mark Lanegan
  and Michael Johnson
Except:
"I Love You, Little Girl"
"Wildflowers"
"Woe"
Published by EMI Blackwood Music,
  Inc.
Words and music by Mark Lanegan
"Juarez"
Published by EMI Blackwood Music,
  Inc.
Words and music by Mark Lanegan
  and Steve Fisk
All Rights Reserved. Used by
  Permission.

Whiskey for the Holy Ghost
All songs published by EMI Black-
  wood Music, Inc.
Words and music by Mark Lanegan
All Rights Reserved. Used by
  Permission.

SINGLE SONGS

"Burning Jacob's Ladder"
Published by Drive Music Publishing
  o/b/o Ripplestick Music
Words and music by Mark Lanegan
All Rights Reserved. Used by
  Permission.

"Black Rider Run"
Published by Drive Music Publishing
  o/b/o Ripplestick Music, Aldo
  Struyf Publishing Designee
Words and music by Mark Lanegan
  and Aldo Struyf
All Rights Reserved. Used by
  Permission.

"Black River"
Published by Drive Music Publishing
  o/b/o Ripplestick Music, Tim
  Simenon Publishing Designee
Words and music by Mark Lanegan
  and Tim Simenon
All Rights Reserved. Used by
  Permission.

"Crawl Like a Dog"
Published by Drive Music Publishing
  o/b/o Ripplestick Music, Aldo
  Struyf Publishing Designee, Tim
  Vanhamel Publishing Designee
Words and music by Mark Lanegan,
  Aldo Struyf, and Tim Vanhamel
All Rights Reserved. Used by
  Permission.

"Gospel"
Published by Drive Music Publishing
  o/b/o Ripplestick Music, Rob
  Marshall Publishing Designee
Words and music by Mark Lanegan
  and Rob Marshall
All Rights Reserved. Used by
  Permission.

"Kingdom"
Published by Drive Music Publishing
  o/b/o Ripplestick Music, Rob
  Marshall Publishing Designee
Words and music by Mark Lanegan
  and Rob Marshall
All Rights Reserved. Used by
  Permission.

"Love Story"
Published by Drive Music Publishing
  o/b/o Ripplestick Music, Black
  Panzer Music
Words and music by Mark Lanegan
  and Mathias Schneeberger
All Rights Reserved. Used by
  Permission.

"Skull"
Published by Drive Music Publishing
  o/b/o Ripplestick Music, Rob
  Marshall Publishing Designee
Words and music by Mark Lanegan
  and Rob Marshall
All Rights Reserved. Used by
  Permission.

"Song #1"
Published by Drive Music Publishing
o/b/o Ripplestick Music, Aldo
Struyf Publishing Designee
Words and music by Mark Lanegan
and Aldo Struyf
All Rights Reserved. Used by
Permission.

"The Monochrome Sun"
Published by Drive Music Publishing
o/b/o Ripplestick Music, Dave
Clarke Publishing Designee
Words and music by Mark Lanegan
and Dave Clarke
All Rights Reserved. Used by
Permission.

"There Is a Serpent Coming"
Published by Drive Music Publishing
o/b/o Ripplestick Music, Dylan
Carlson Publishing Designee
Words and music by Mark Lanegan
and Dylan Carlson
All Rights Reserved. Used by
Permission.

"Untitled Lullaby"
Published by Drive Music Publishing
o/b/o Ripplestick Music
Words and music by Mark Lanegan
All Rights Reserved. Used by
Permission.

"Another Night Out"
Published by Drive Music Publishing
o/b/o Ripplestick Music, Kobalt
Music Publishing, Hosmer Music

Words and music by Mark Lanegan,
James Lavelle, Pablo Clements,
and James Griffith
All Rights Reserved. Used by
Permission.

"Mirrored"
Published by EMI Blackwood Music,
Inc.
Words and music by Mark Lanegan
All Rights Reserved. Used by
Permission.

"Mud Pink Skag"
Published by EMI Blackwood Music,
Inc.
Words and music by Mark Lanegan
All Rights Reserved. Used by
Permission.

"Revolver"
Published by EMI Blackwood Music,
Inc.
Words and music by Mark Lanegan
All Rights Reserved. Used by
Permission.

"Staring Down the Dust"
Published by Drive Music Publishing
o/b/o Ripplestick Music, Stupid-
ditties Music, Theory of Color,
Channel This Music, Loss Leader
Music
Words and music by Mark Lanegan,
Ben Shepherd, Matt Cameron,
Alain Johannes, and Dimitri Coats
All Rights Reserved. Used by
Permission.

Index